WEAPONS
OF WAR

This book was devised and produced by
Multimedia Publications (UK) Ltd.

Editor: Jeff Groman
Design: John Strange and Associates
Picture Research: Military Archive &
Research Services – John & Diane Moore.
Contributors: Hugh W. Cowin, Charles
Messenger, Chris Chant
Production: Arnon Orbach

ISBN 0 8317 9384 8

First published in the United States of
America 1985 by Gallery Books, an imprint of
W. H. Smith Publishers Inc., 112 Madison
Avenue, New York, NY 10016

Typeset by Flowery Typesetters Ltd.
Origination D.S. Colour International Ltd.
Printed in Italy by Sagdos, Milan.

These pages: By air to battle: UH-1H
helicopters of the US Army.

WEAPONS OF WAR

Edited by Jeff Groman

GALLERY BOOKS
An Imprint of W. H. Smith Publishers Inc.
112 Madison Avenue
New York City 10016

These Pages: General Dynamics
F-16 Fighting Falcon.

CONTENTS

United States battleship Iowa tries
its 16 inch guns on Korea, 1952.

Introduction

At the start of this century the naval cruiser represented the most awesome single weapon in existence. On the broader front of naval warfare planning, old ideas still reigned supreme, with little in sight to threaten the type of surface action so familiar to naval officers since the days of Sir Francis Drake. Few but the most far-sighted naval planners could have imagined the fundamental shifts which naval warfare and its vessels would undergo as the world entered the twentieth century.

Old theories under attack

The first major new development to be widely accepted by the world's navies, in the years immediately preceding World War I, was the submarine. From then on, new weapons of naval warfare followed one upon another, with the bitter period of the 1914–18 War providing the major impetus. By 1918, navies throughout the world were being compelled to face the new threats of the submarine, the contact mine and the aircraft. Britain, previously one of the most conservative of the leading naval powers, introduced the world's first purpose-built aircraft carrier in the shape of the HMS *Argus.*

The interwar years

After World War I, the Washington Treaty was introduced, aimed at limiting the size, firepower and number of battleships possessed by any one nation. It was a time to turn swords into ploughshares. Meanwhile, Britain and Japan, among others, sought ways to get around the legislation and worked secretly to outflank the Treaty limitations. As the 1920s drew to a close, the leading navies of the world, including Britain and the US, began to accept the aircraft carrier in place of the battleship as their capital naval asset.

From the early 1930s onwards the race to re-arm was spearheaded by a massive increase in the size of the world's leading navies, especially those of Germany and Japan. Germany, who had learned more than most about the use of submarine warfare from World War I, began a program of submarine construction on a huge scale.

In the mid-1930s Britain developed ASDIC, an acoustic aid to underwater detection, which was hastily fitted to most Royal Navy surface combatants and generally held to be the final solution to the submarine problem. ASDIC's limitations were later to be exposed, as U-Boat commanders were able to mask their movements by running on the surface, where wave noise worked very much to their advantage.

The impact of air power

The 1940s saw aircraft making a major impact on the shape of naval operations and the kind of warships required.

The first major air/sea actions of World War II were mounted by Japan with their massive surprise carrier-based air attacks on Pearl Harbor and its neighboring airfields. Six months later, it was the turn of the Japanese to suffer at the hands of air strikes from mainly US Navy carrierborne squadrons during the crucial Battle of Midway.

The dropping of the atomic bombs, in August 1945, on the Japanese cities of Hiroshima and Nagasaki, and the terrible devastation it caused, did more than accelerate the end of World War II. It also cast a question mark over the whole future of large naval task groups of the kind that had proven so indispensable to the conduct of the US campaign in the Pacific. For more than the next decade the major navies of the world found themselves to be the poor relations of their air forces when it came to share out the national defense budgetary cake.

Towards today

The re-emergence of the world's leading navies to something of their former glory began with the US Navy's pioneering of nuclear propulsion, first for hunter/killer submarines, and then in cruisers and aircraft carriers. Nuclear propulsion represented a major breakthrough in naval operational terms by providing a vessel with virtually unlimited range.

In the early 1960s, the US Navy closed the circle with their development of the submarine-carried intercontinental ballistic missile: a pattern to be followed by the Soviet Union, Britain, France and the Peoples' Republic of China. Today, with fixed, land-based ballistic missiles vulnerable to pre-emptive strike, the use of submarine-launched ballistic missiles has thrust the world's navies back into the forefront of national strategic nuclear-armed forces. Equally important has been the introduction of the ship-launched anti-ship missile, which has had a dramatic impact on navies worldwide and the kind of vessels they operate. Generally, this weapon has equalized the firepower available to navies large and small, with aircraft carriers and battleships having to guard against long-range missile attack from small, agile fast attack craft that are less readily detectable than a larger ship.

Left The Canadian Navy's HMCS *Ojibwa* (SS72), one of three modified British-developed Oberon class diesel-electric boats.

Below left The lead of this French Navy class of 16 ballistic missile-carrying nuclear-powered submarines is *Le Redoubtable.* Seven have been ordered.

Right HMS *Swiftsure* (S126), first of this six boat Royal Navy nuclear-powered hunter/killer class. All entered service between 1973 and 1981.

Far right HMS *Turbulent* (S114), second of this Royal Navy five boat Trafalgar class nuclear-powered hunter/killer submarines.

Submarines and aircraft carriers

The present generation of submarines can be grouped under two types: nuclear-powered and diesel-electric powered. The first type includes ballistic missile launchers and hunter/killer types used to hunt other hostile submarines. The role of diesel-electric powered submarines is mainly that of hunter/killer, with a useful secondary mission capability of attacking hostile surface vessels that may enter their patrol area. All types of submarines employed today still carry torpedoes, giving them some varying degree of both anti-submarine and anti-ship capability.

In recent years the modern nuclear-powered submarines – and especially the intercontinental ballistic missile launchers – have tended to steal much of the limelight, but diesel-electric boats still have a future. Indeed, not only is the quiet-running diesel-electric submarine valued by smaller navies, but new classes of such vessels are being built or are on order for all of the world's major navies except the US.

The power of the aircraft carrier

The aircraft carriers of today can also be grouped under two main types: the large, conventional aircraft-catapulting type of which the US Navy operates both nuclear-powered and steam turbine driven classes; and the much more compact jump jet and helicopter operating carriers, typified by the Royal Navy's Invincible class and Soviet Navy's Kiev class ships.

The typically large US Navy carrier can carry between 70 and 90 planes giving a single carrier a global range air strike capacity greater than most of the world's air forces. Significantly, the Soviet Navy has recently elected to follow the same path and is currently building a 75,000 ton plus carrier of their own.

Battleships, cruisers and destroyers

The battleship's heyday was during the late 1930s and the very early 1940s, as typified by Japan's Yamato class mammoth battlewagons. Indeed, no battleship has been launched anywhere in the world since the USS *Kentucky* was launched in January 1950. The US Navy has clung grimly to its four completed Iowa class ships, periodically bringing one or more of them out of mothballs as late as 1969 to provide heavy shore bombardment support off the coast of Vietnam. During the latter half of the 1970s, to many people's surprise, the US Navy revealed plans to modernize and refurbish all four battleships. The first two are now back in full operation.

These veritable floating fortresses have retained their big 16-inch gun batteries, but these are now complemented by a formidable mix of Harpoon anti-ship and Tomahawk cruise missiles. As well as being heavily armed, these ships are also heavily armor clad, and have a much greater chance of surviving a strike by bomb or missile than do the far more fragile later warships.

The superpower cruiser

The cruiser, once the principal surface ship employed by the large majority of navies, is rapidly becoming a luxury only affordable by the two superpower navies of the US and the Soviet Union. The types of cruisers being built in the two countries, however, are very different. The US has opted for the relatively light Ticonderoga class anti-aircraft ships, while Soviet cruisers, of which there are a growing number of classes, tend to be more general-purpose in terms of mission, as well as bigger and heavier.

The growth of the destroyers

The destroyer started life at around the turn of the century as a relatively small, light and agile ship designed to counter the threat from the fast torpedo boat. However, since the early 1940s, the destroyer has become more closely identified with an anti-aircraft role. Over the past 30 years or so, the size and weight of the destroyer has crept up from around 2,500 tons to between 4,500 tons and nearly 8,000 tons. Virtually all of the modern destroyers are gas turbine-propelled, but because of their greater weight have top speeds of around 30 knots as against the 35 or more knot capability of their World War II forebears.

Frigates and corvettes

The term frigate was for long associated in both US and French minds with the destroyer leader or light cruiser. It now generally means an ocean-going ship whose primary mission is to counter the submarine threat. Although still carrying the shipboard torpedoes and anti-submarine mortars of their ancestors, modern frigates place most of their operational reliance on their ship-stowed anti-submarine helicopters. As with the modern destroyers, today's frigates are almost universally gas turbine-powered, but in some cases employ diesels for fuel economy reasons when operating at lower speeds. Many of the world's frigates carry a useful anti-ship missile armament.

Above USS *Michigan* (SSBN727), second of this planned 15 boat Ohio class. Each of these nuclear-powered vessels carry 24 Trident ballistic missiles and is almost as long as a Virginia class cruiser.

Right The *Sauro*, lead boat of this six vessel Italian Navy patrol class.

Above An F-4 Phantom II being
launched from the deck of the
USS *Constellation* (CV64), a Kitty
Hawk class carrier.

Below The steam turbine-
powered USS *Kitty Hawk* (CV63),
first of a four carrier class that
includes the modified USS *John F
Kennedy* (CV67). All carry an 85
plane air group.

Left USS *Carl Vinson* (CVN70), third of the six carrier Nimitz class nuclear-powered mammoths, each with a 90 plane air group.

The versatile corvette

The corvette is generally designed either for general-purpose duties or as an anti-submarine supplement to the larger frigate. It was used in great numbers by the Allied Powers during World War II's Battle of the Atlantic, but appeared to drop from favor during the 1950s and 1960s, and only re-emerged in popularity at the beginning of the 1970s. As endurance, rather than high dash speeds, are a major design feature of most modern corvettes, the primary propulsion usually chosen is the diesel, although both US and Dutch corvette constructors have employed gas turbines for ships they supplied to Saudi Arabia and Indonesia respectively. The latest Italian-developed Esmeraldas class corvettes of 700 tons are capable of deploying a respectably-sized AB212ASW helicopter from their elevated aft helipad platform. Many modern corvettes carry anti-ship missiles.

Fast attack and patrol vessels

The small, agile fast attack craft has been around in one form or another since the 1890s. Up to the mid-1960s, primary offensive armament had been the 21-inch heavyweight torpedo employed as an anti-surface ship weapon. However, thanks largely to the Soviet-led development of the relatively lightweight ship-launched anti-ship missile, the current generation of fast attack craft have been given the same firepower potency as that of warships many times their size. Historically, the Germans have tended to excel in the design and development of these types and it should therefore come as no surprise to find the West German boatbuilders maintaining dominance in the fast attack craft markets worldwide. Interestingly, the 1960s and early 1970s courtship between the fast attack craft designer and the gas turbine engine appears to be on the wane, with most of the more recently designed craft exploiting the fuel economies offered by the new breed of diesel engines.

Below The *Garibaldi*, first aircraft carrier to join the Italian Navy, can operate Harrier/Sea Harrier jump jets if required.

The role of the patrol vessel

The patrol vessel category covers a variety of ships and craft ranging from the very modern breed of 1,200 ton ocean-going patrol and fishery protection vessels, to 30 or 40 ton inshore patrol boats employed in river or harbor policing duties.

After the mid-1970s internationally agreed extensions of national territorial water limits out to 200 nautical miles from shore, there emerged a market for economic and effective specialized offshore patrol vessels. Britain was the first in the field with its Royal Navy's Island class. Following on from this, the Royal Navy has taken delivery of two somewhat larger Castle class ships and is in the course of accepting five Peacock class patrol vessels for use in Hong Kong waters. Spain also has produced a new offshore patrol vessel, equipped with a helicopter platform aft, and has already sold five of this class to Argentina and another six to Mexico.

Support vessels

This chapter covers a fairly wide variety of non-combatant vessels ranging from the vast, latterday US Navy's Tarawa class assault ships, through the vital underway replenishers, to minehunters and landing craft: all of which play a largely unsung but crucial role in the overall scheme of naval operations.

The modern assault ship, typified by the Tarawa class in the US and the Soviets' Ivan Rogov class vessels, is a far cry from the very standard commercial cargo and troopship designs employed during World War II. All modern assault ships carry a sizable helicopter-operating platform from which their marine infantry can lift off, while the below deck space carries a vast volume of fighting equipment, ammunition and other provisions. Most modern assault ships are equipped with a floodable well deck astern, enabling them to house and disembark up to tank-carrying-sized landing craft.

Below The *Jean De Vienne* (D643), fourth of this ultimate seven ship French Navy destroyer class, of which *George Leygues* (D640) is the lead ship.

Right The impressively armed Italian Navy cruiser *Vittorio Veneto,* following her recent refit and looking every inch a warship.

Left HMS *Glasgow* (D88), sixth and last of the Royal Navy's Type 42 Batch I Sheffield class guided missile destroyers.

Below USS *Mississippi* (CGN40), third of this four ship nuclear-powered cruiser class used primarily as carrier escorts.

Above USS *Elliott* (DDG967), one of the US Navy's 31 ship Spruance class gas turbine-powered guided missile destroyers.

Center Japan's *Shirane* (DDH143), the first of this 12 ship helicopter-carrying destroyer class. Note the vast helipad area aft.

Left USS *Ticonderoga* (CG47), first of this planned 18 ship gas turbine-powered area air defense cruiser class.

Minesweepers and their successors

The present-day mine countermeasures vessel has also come a long way from the relatively simple minesweepers of World War II. Today's minehunters can still be operated in pairs or teams to clear a channel through a sown field of conventional mines, but they need more than one trick up their sleeve to counter the more clever, electronically controlled devices that are becoming increasingly common. To combat these, the modern minehunter is designed to offer the minimum magnetic, sound and pressure indications of its presence during operation. Equipped with high-definition sonar, the minehunter slowly advances to within safe range of an unidentified underwater target. A small, remotely-controlled submersible is then launched from the minehunter to inspect the target at close quarters. If the target does turn out to be some form of mine, the submersible leaves a destructive charge close to the mine and withdraws back to its mother ship. An operator on board then triggers the charge and destroys the mine. If for any reason it needs to retrieve the mine for subsequent inspection, the minehunter dispatches a team of naval divers to bring the device aboard.

Significantly, the US Navy, which has tended to neglect its surface mine countermeasures assets over the past 30 or so years, has now embarked on two major minehunter programs: one to counter the deepwater, anti-submarine mine; the other to combat shallow seabed or tethered mines.

Tanker support

The part played today by the underway replenisher or fleet oiler in naval operations any distance from base cannot be overstated. Without these vital fuel and supply-laden workhorses, the tactical operational radius of a task group's action could be counted in hundreds, rather than thousands, of miles. Indeed, as the recent experience of the Royal Navy's South Atlantic Task Force showed, no British repossession of the Falklands could ever have been contemplated without the tanker support provided by the ships of the Royal Fleet Auxiliary. Significantly, the Soviets, after many years of relying upon their merchant tanker and cargo-carrying fleet to resupply active naval units, have turned to the development of naval replenishers to help extend the range of their fighting ships.

Landing craft

All too often overlooked by armchair strategists, the landing craft comes into its own when the need arises to put troops ashore or resupply beach-head forces with loads too heavy to be ferried in by helicopter. Ironically, despite Britain's pioneering development of the air cushion, or hovercraft, it was the Soviet navy that was to produce a family of air cushion landing craft. The largest of these can speed 220 trooops or a mix of troops and main battle tanks over the water and far beyond the beach at speeds in excess of 40 miles per hour.

HMCS *Iroquois* (DDH280), first of this four ship Canadian Navy destroyer class, mainly operating in the North Atlantic.

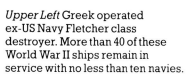

Upper Left Greek operated ex-US Navy Fletcher class destroyer. More than 40 of these World War II ships remain in service with no less than ten navies.

Lower Left The *Haruna* (DDH141), lead of this two ship Japanese destroyer class, which, like the Shirane class, are primarily sub killers.

Top HMS *Beaver* (F93), second of the Royal Navy's six ship stretched Batch II Broadsword class gas turbine-powered frigates.

Above and Upper Right Forward and aft views of HMS *Broadsword* (F88), the first of four Type 22 Royal Navy frigates.

Center Right The *Banckert* (F810), the fourth of the 12 Dutch-built and operated Kortenaer class frigates.

Right The *Tromp* (F801), lead of this two ship Royal Netherlands Navy frigate class.

Above Far Left The Italian lead of class gas turbine-powered frigate *Lupo* (F564) and her three sister ships were all delivered between 1977 and 1980.

Above Center Not normally operated in such close company are these three US Navy Sperry class frigates comprising from front to rear USS *Jack Williams* (F24), USS *Antrim* (F20) and USS *Sperry* (F07).

Above Britain's Royal Navy operates eight Leander class frigates modified to mount the Ikara anti-submarine missile, including HMS *Aurora* (F10) shown here.

Left Italy's Lupo class is the most widely exported of all modern frigates, with 14 sales. Shown here is the Venezuelan Navy's *Jose Felix Ribas* (F26).

Right HMS *Amazon* (F169), lead of this original eight ship Royal Navy frigate class, two of which were lost to heavy Argentinian air attacks while serving in Falklands Sound.

Below The *Skudd* (P967), one of the 19 Storm class remaining in Norwegian service, seen unleashing a Penguin anti-ship missile.

Far Right Top The Canadian frigate HMCS *Sauguenag* (F206), eldest of this six ship helicopter-carrying St. Laurent class.

Far Right Bottom The *Liberal* (F43) is the fourth of Brazil's six ship Niteroi class frigates designed in Britain, where four were built.

Right Despite its small size, *Esmeraldas* (CM11), lead of this six Ecuadorian corvette class, built in Italy, can operate a sizeable anti-submarine helicopter from its aft helipad.

F169

206

F43

Right One of the ten Federal
German Navy missle armed,
Lurssen-designed Type 143A
fast attack craft.

Left The Royal Danish Navy operates three of these Niels Juel class corvettes. Shown here is the lead ship, F354.

Below The Omani Navy's *Dhofar* (B10), first of the three craft Province class designed and built in Britain.

Above USS *Hercules* (PHM2), the second of this five craft US Navy missile-armed Pegasus fast attack hydrofoil class.

Left A French-built Combattante III class missile craft, this particular vessel being the Greek *Simaiforos Kavalouthis* (P24).

Far Left An informative view of the Federal German Navy's lead of class frigate *Bremen* (F207). The Bremen class uses the Dutch-developed Kortenaer class hull and same general layout, but employs US rather than British gas turbines as its prime propulsion. Six ships have been completed, but more may be ordered.

Below Left The *Terne* (P988), third of this Royal Norwegian Navy 14 craft Hawk class firing a Penguin anti-ship missile.

Below Right The *Dogan* (P340), lead of this Turkish Navy operated class of Lurssen-designed Type FPB57 missile craft.

Lower The Norwegians operate six Snogg class fast attack craft, this one being *Rapp* (P981), the second to be built.

Right One of the Egyptian Navy's six craft, missile-equipped Ramadan class at speed.

P 981

Above The *Hammer* (P542), one of ten Willemoes class fast attack craft belonging to the Royal Danish Navy.

Center Left Italy operates seven of these OTOMAT anti-ship missile-armed Sparviero class fast attach hydrofoils.

Right The *Cazadora* (F35), fifth of Spain's eight Descubierta class corvettes. Egypt and Morocco also operate this type.

Lower Right Bahrain's *P11*, second of this two craft Lurssen FPB38 design class, each armed with two single 40mm Breda/Bofors guns.

Left Two Swedish Navy Spica class fast attack craft, of which there are six, demonstrating their impressive turn of speed.

Top Right Argentina ordered five of these Spanish designed and built Halcon class patrol vessels. Seen here is the lead Argentinian ship, *Mantilla* (GC24).

Above HMS *Peacock* (P239), first of this latest Royal Navy five patrol vessel class is fitted with a rapid fire OTO-Melara 76mm gun.

Below Right Italy's Sparviero class fast attack hydrofoil developed under a joint programme with the US.

Below The Royal Navy's HMS *Leeds Castle* (P258), lead ship of this two patrol vessel class.

Right The Japanese minelayer *Soya* (MMC951) can lay six lanes of mines simultaneously.

Center Right The *Var* (A608), third of this French Navy four ship Durance class underway replenisher, also ordered by Australia.

Below Left The Italian Navy's *Lerici* (M5550), the first of this new minehunter class also ordered by Indonesia, Nigeria and Malaysia, accounting for 20 sales by late 1984.

Above Right Japan's *Narushima* (M657), ninth of the Hatsushima class mine-hunters.

Center Right HMS *Waveney* (M2003), the first of this 12 ship deep water minesweeper class being delivered to the Royal Navy.

Below Right HMS *Cattistock* (M31), leading HMS *Ledbury* (M30), two of the Royal Navy's Hunt class minehunters. 11 of these very capable ships have been ordered by late 1984.

Right The Dutch fleet
replenisher, HNLMS *Zuiderkruis*
(A832).

Left One of the six British Hovercraft Wellington class patrol/landing craft sold to Iran prior to the overthrow of the Shah.

Above A Soviet Navy Aist class landing craft. Clearly visible are the aircraft-style propellers used for propulsion.

The F-16 Fighting Falcon.

AIRCRAFT

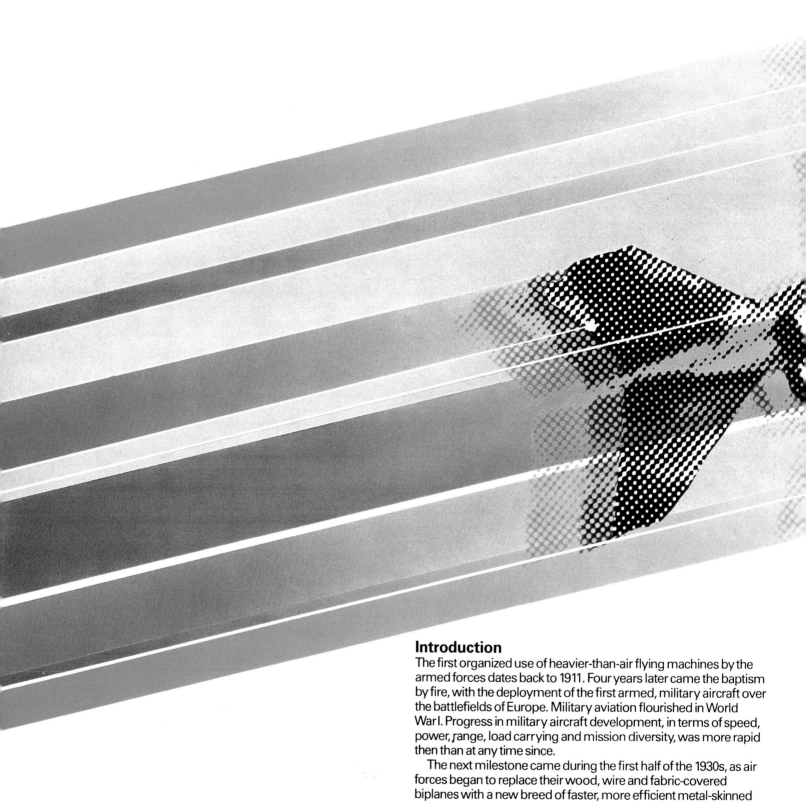

Introduction

The first organized use of heavier-than-air flying machines by the armed forces dates back to 1911. Four years later came the baptism by fire, with the deployment of the first armed, military aircraft over the battlefields of Europe. Military aviation flourished in World War I. Progress in military aircraft development, in terms of speed, power, range, load carrying and mission diversity, was more rapid then than at any time since.

The next milestone came during the first half of the 1930s, as air forces began to replace their wood, wire and fabric-covered biplanes with a new breed of faster, more efficient metal-skinned monoplanes. In Germany, Hitler set about building the most modern air force of the time. Its awesome power was demonstrated when the Condor Legion bombers were enlisted in support of General Franco during the Spanish Civil War. At about the same time, Japan and Italy, Germany's allies during World War II, used air power with crushing effect in their colonial wars in China and Ethiopia.

The coming of the jet

World War II bolstered the image and standing of air power, but brought surprisingly few gains in terms of military aircraft development. By 1940, Germany, Italy, Britain and the US were all working on the development of jet-powered aircraft, but only Britain and Germany were to field jet aircraft, in small numbers, towards the end of the war. The first large-scale deployment of jet fighters in war, came several years later, during the Korean War, when American F-86 Sabres were confronted by Soviet developed MiG-15s.

At the start of the 1950s, only a handful of military research aircraft had penetrated the sonic barrier, but by the end of the decade, numerous combat pilots, mostly American, were routinely flying at twice the speed of sound. It was also in the late fifties that the intercontinental ballistic missile made its appearance and superseded the bomber as the most potent weapon in the military arsenal.

High technology vs. low cost

The next fifteen years or so provided plenty of opportunity to exercise air power, in places as far afield as Cuba and Vietnam. From the standpoint of military aircraft evolution, technology offered more than ever before, Britain's Harrier jump jet and the American Mach 3 SR-71 being two examples. But high technology was expensive, and many of the more ambitious military aircraft programs had to be curtailed. Taking advantage of this, Northrop in the US and Dassault in France both developed reasonably cheap, easy-to-operate fighters, the F-5 and Mirage III, and successfully sold them to air forces worldwide.

Since then, there has been a trend towards buying lower-priced, multi-mission machines, such as the new breed of light jet or turboprop-powered strike/trainers. Nevertheless, tactical air power remains as important today as it ever was, as was shown during the recent conflict between Britain and Argentina over the Falkland Islands.

Gladiators of the Skies

For young and old alike, the fighter aircraft and its pilot have always held a special fascination. They represent an image of the ultimate challenge in man's control over machine, spiced by more than a hint of gladiatorial danger never too far away.

A technological transformation

The machines have evolved tremendously over the past 75 years. Since 1915 speeds have risen from something like those of a modest modern motor car to top speeds in excess of 1500 mph at altitude, or over 750 mph in the denser air at low level.

The lethality of today's fighter is awesome. Through the widespread adoption of the missile, coupled with airborne radar, the modern fighter can destroy its unseen prey often at distances well beyond the visual acquisition range of the pilot's eye. Another major advantage of today's fighters is their greatly extended radius of action, made possible by the use of in-flight refueling. With air-to-air refueling now routinely provided by tanker aircraft, the duration of a fighter pilot's sortie has leapt from not much more than an hour to the limits of the individual's endurance.

Since the mid-1950s the performance of the fighter has surged ahead on almost every front. Combat experience gained in South East Asia and the Middle East has shown that, despite the introduction of longer-ranged missile armament aboard fighters, the need for a fighter to be able to engage in close range 'dogfighting' with one or more of the enemy is as great as ever. The fighter designer must continue to provide his machine with the highest degree of combat agility. In consequence, the modern fighter has grown more high-lift-inducing devices, including inboard wing leading edge extensions, flaps and slats, than was conceivable 20 years ago.

Weapons systems

In South East Asia the US Air Force found that the effectiveness of their F-4 Phantom II's all-missile armament was limited. This led to a hasty program to retrofit the aircraft with an internally mounted, multi-barreled 20mm gun system. Every fighter design that has emerged since then has incorporated some form of internally mounted gun armament to complement its missile fit.

With most non-Warsaw Pact air arms, two families of missiles, in particular, the AIM-7 Sparrow and the AIM-9 Sidewinder, have become standard. These weapons, which were first evolved at the start of the 1950s, may not have changed significantly in their outward appearance over the years, but they have been subject to internal guidance and other systems development on an intensive scale.

Both were originally developed for the US Navy. The beyond-20-mile-ranging Sparrow, with its radar homing head, was devised to counter the incoming bomber threat; while the shorter-ranged Sidewinder, with its heat-seeking homing head, started life as a weapon to be launched from behind its prey over ranges from half a mile to around two and a half miles. Both missiles are now far more lethal and can operate in a wider range of conditions that take account of weather and potential enemy countermeasures. The range of the latest Sidewinders has been extended to around nine miles.

44

Top One of the USA's latest fighters, the Northrop Tigershark.

Above Left A US Navy F-4G landing back aboard. The unusual Navy color scheme helped conceal the machine during overland 'Wild Weasel' missions aimed at locating and destroying enemy radar and missile defenses.

Left McDonnell's legendary F-4 Phantom II provides the strike fighter backbone of numerous air forces while remaining in service with its original clients, the US Navy and Marine Corps. Seen here is a Navy F-4B.

Above The US Navy's potent, 2-seat, twin-engined, all-weather Grumman F-14A Tomcat, depicted here carrying a mix of AIM-7 Sparrows and AIM-9 Sidewinder air-to-air missiles.

Performance and cost

The current range of fighters comprises three distinct tiers, separated by capability and cost. At the top are the high-capability F-14 Tomcat, F-15 Eagle and Panavia Tornado F2, which each cost anything from $30 million upwards. Next, come the newer generation types such as the F-16 Fighting Falcon, F-18 Hornet and Mirage 2000, each carrying a price tag of around $20 million. The third tier comprises the F-5E Tiger II, Mirage 50 and F1, plus the recently developed F-20, all costing between $8 million and $15 million.

Bombers and Strike Aircraft

The large long-ranged bomber aircraft made its debut in 1916, but its effectiveness as a strategic weapon was not demonstrated until World War II. For the next ten years, the bomber reigned supreme as the means of delivering megaton destruction from the skies over virtually any city or target. By the mid-1950s, however, the bomber's brief heyday seemed to be over, with the arrival of the even more potent and unstoppable intercontinental ballistic missile.

In search of a role

During the 1960s and 1970s, the bomber came to be seen as an anachronism that only the US and USSR could afford – as a backup to their strategic missile armories. Apart from the superpowers, only France clung to the manned bomber concept, developing the Mirage IV for deployment with its strategic nuclear forces.

Even the US, with its vast resources of money and technology, was losing the capability to develop new bombers. First the supersonic B-58 Hustler ran into insuperable technical problems; then its projected follow-up, the XB-70, was shelved; and finally, the program to develop the ambitious B-1, begun in 1970 by the US Air Force, was canceled in 1977 because of escalating costs.

The new B-1B, resurrected in 1980, is a more radically modified aircraft than its outward appearance would suggest. Apart from its improved ability to penetrate defended air space at low level, virtually every other sector of its performance, compared with the original B-1, has been reduced.

Only the Soviets, with the Tu-22 'Blinder' and Tu-22M 'Backfire', appear able to produce new bombers. Designed around a primary anti-shipping role, they would operate at higher altitudes, known to be much kindlier to airframes and engines.

Acquiring missile capability

Today's bomber either has to remain undetected by the enemy, or must be able to release its weapons far enough away from heavily defended targets to avoid being shot down. The Soviets have expended much effort in developing 'stand-off' missiles, which can be air-launched from their parent bomber platforms up to nearly 400 miles from target.

Around the mid-1970s, both the US Navy and Air Force belatedly turned their attention to the development of the cruise missile, leading to the Navy's BGM-109 Tomahawk and Air Force's AGM-86. The introduction of the AGM-86, with a range of 1500 miles, has greatly extended the usefulness of the veteran B-52 Stratofortress. The deployment of the air-launched variant of the BGM-109 Tomahawk aboard the US Navy's A-6 Intruder and P-3 Orion aircraft will likewise dramatically increase their strike range.

Right Despite its early 1950s origin, the Hawker Hunter still remains in widespread use, with over 450, including this Swiss Air Force example, still in service.

Top Left An F-14A of Fighting Squadron Two with its swivelling wings moved fully back, the position adopted for high speed flight.

Second Left This Fighting Thirty Second F-14A carries six AIM-54 Phoenix air-to-air missiles, each of which can be simultaneously directed at its own target.

Third Left A long range AIM-54 Phoenix missile boosts away from this F-14A of Navy Fighting Squadron Two-Eleven.

Bottom Left These two US Air Force F-4E fighter bombers carry Pave Tack weapon aiming equipment, visible beneath the fuselage immediately below the pilot's position.

Upper Right A French Air Force Dassault Mirage III, illustrious sire of this mainly delta winged family. This particular aircraft carries a Martel air-to-ground missile.

Right Dassault's Mirage F1 departs from the company's tailless delta wing formula. The F1's orderbook exceeds 690 aircraft.

Top The more powerfully engined Mirage 5 represents the ultimate in direct Mirage III development. Total orders for this Mirage III and 5 family exceeds 1,410.

Above A four plane formation of single seat, twin-engined McDonnell F-15A Eagles, the US Air Force's premier all-weather fighter.

Strike aircraft

From 1967 onwards the effective use of Soviet-built ground-based air defense missile and gun systems in the Middle East conflicts has done much to influence the way strike aircraft operate. These experiences showed that to be successful, a modern strike aircraft had to be capable of approaching its target as low and fast as possible. Electronics to guide the pilot unerringly towards the target and to compute the precise release point for his weapons on his first and only pass are also now considered essential. These latest developments have to some degree relieved the strike aircraft designer's problems; but only for the larger, more powerful strike types, capable of lofting not only such missiles as the AGM-65 Maverick, but the necessary aircraft-carried control and guidance electronics. This limits the adoption of such mission-enhancing systems to aircraft of the size of the A-4 Skyhawk, Hawker Hunter and above. It also distinguishes between the strike aircraft employable over major battle zones and the lighter strike types suited to missions against less heavily defended targets.

The growing size and deployment of the Soviet fleets over the past two decades have led to the development of the large maritime patrol and strike aircraft. Recently, missiles such as the AGM-84 Harpoon (with its range of up to 60 miles), have extended mission capability, adding an anti-ship punch to their primary anti-submarine warfare role.

Above The 2-seat F-15B Eagle is used to introduce new pilots to this highly agile aircraft, but retains a full fighting capability.

Below Although almost contemporary to the Hunter, many Lockheed F-104G Starfighters remain in use with a number of air forces, this example serving with the Greek Air Force.

Light Attack and Trainers

Despite the need to produce adequately trained pilots, the training aircraft was generally neglected by many air arms throughout the 1950s and 1960s. Even the larger air forces tended to use as trainers, adaptations of designs originally intended for more pressing operational roles. The widely used T-33, for example, was a two-seat version of the F-80 Shooting Star. Still today, the more advanced flying training of transport and maritime patrol pilots is usually undertaken on barely modified versions of standard airliner or business aviation types, such as the Jetstream, used by both the RAF and Royal Navy.

There were a few exceptions to the practice of allocating low priorities to the procurement of training aircraft, among them the US's supersonic T-38 and Britain's agile, load-hauling Hawk.

Life-cycle costing

The real shift started slowly in the late 1960s and early 1970s, but the change was largely confined to the US and major European air arms, which were looking to husband their flying fuel costs in order to purchase more operational aircraft. With government constraints on service spending, more and more air arms look at their purchases in terms of life-cycle costs, a concept that takes in not only the capital outlay to buy the aircraft, but also its cost to fly and maintain. Today, factors such as fuel economy could well outweigh an aircraft's somewhat higher initial price tag when compared with a more fuel hungry rival. If a service can save on any aspect of operating costs, these savings can be translated into additional funding for new equipment purchases.

The change to turbo

Although the oil price rises of the 1970s had a significant impact on both the price and production of gasoline – used by piston-engined aircraft – aviation turbine fuel, kerosene, was not so profoundly affected. Almost instantly, the turbine and turboprop engine became very popular, particularly in the many countries affected by oil refinery closures.

The aircraft manufacturers were quick to respond. A number of companies either re-engined existing trainer designs to turboprop power or, as in the case of Brazil's EMB-312 Tucano, initiated a new breed of light strike/trainer aircraft designed around the turboprop engine from the outset.

The last five or six years have been characterized by a sharp increase in the numbers of light jets such as the Hawk and Alpha Jet, and turboprop types, such as the EMB-312, PC-7 Turbo Trainer and the T-34C Turbo Mentor.

Above The single-engined General Dynamics F-16A Fighting Falcon is operated by the US Air Force and those of numerous other nations. This four plane formation (of which three are shown here) belongs to the US Air Force's 474th Tactical Fighter Wing, based at Nellis Air Force Base, Nevada.

Below Inspecting an F-15A radar antenna dish, the size of which indicates a powerful, long range search and track capability. Note also the cavernous left-side engine air intake.

Right The twin-engined Mirage 4000, like the smaller Mirage 2000, employs latterday 'fly-by-wire' flying controls.

Left A 2-seat F-16B launching an AGM-65 Maverick air-to-ground missile.

Right F-16As of the US Air Force's 388th Tactical Fighter Wing on the flight line at Hill Air Force Base, Utah. More than 1,350 F-16 had been built, both in the US and Europe, by the end of 1984.

Right An F-18A Hornet aboard the carrier USS *Constellation.* Note the lengthy strakes extending forward from the inboard wing and incorporated to improve the type's dog fighting abilities.

Vital Transport and Support

Despite the long-standing US domination of the military transport aircraft scene, the first such machines were of British origin. Introduced in March 1918, the first example of the military transport was a cabin conversion of the DH 4 light bomber. Britain remained one of the leading proponents of military transport aircraft operations throughout the next two decades, largely because of her need to move personnel and supplies over the long-range routes to Africa, the Middle East and India.

It was America however, who developed the first, if somewhat crude, form of in-flight refueling system in order to make the initial non-stop flight across the USA in February 1923. By the mid-1930s,

Soviet and German-led use of paratroopers helped further extend the scope of military air transport operations.

World War II provided a massive spur to military air transport operations and production, especially within the US. Britain was mainly preoccupied with the task of developing and producing fighters and bombers. This helped set the seal on post-war dominance in this field by the US.

The arrival of the Hercules

During the 1930s and 1940s, most of the military transport aircraft in service worldwide could trace their ancestry to that of a preceding Junkers, Ford or Douglas airliner. However, by the late 1940s, the

Left The McDonnell F/A-18A Hornet, a twin-engined, single seat multi-mission strike fighter, designed to replace the A-4, A-7 and F-4 in both US Navy and Marine Corps service, has also been selected for use by Australia, Canada and Spain.

Below Dassault's latest, the single-engined, single-seat Mirage 2000 carries on the French tradition of building fast, agile, easy to fly fighters, clearly pitched to have broad export appeal.

large, heavy transcontinental or intercontinental airliners being developed were finding their operations ever more limited to long, reinforced runways and were clearly incapable of flying in and out of rough, unimproved airstrips. Thus, towards the close of the 1940s, the US in particular committed increasing effort to the development of rough field-compatible, tactical transport types, suitable for assault or battlefield re-supply work.

When, in August 1952, the C-130 Hercules made its debut, few could possibly have realized then that this plane would come to be viewed as the standard transport workhorse of air arms throughout the Non-Eastern Bloc world, let alone that it would still be being produced at a rate of 36 aircraft a year in 1984!

Development of in-flight refueling

During the late 1940s and early 1950s, the US started to resurrect their interest in air-to-air refueling. This would mean short-ranged fighter and strike aircraft units could be deployed faster to distant points around the globe. In-flight refueling was used aboard tanker conversions of the B-50 and C-97 piston-engined aircraft that preceded the jet-powered KC-135, which appeared in the mid-1950s.

Although there have been larger and heavier transports developed for the US Air Force since the C-130 and KC-135, including the C-141 Starlifter and C-5 Galaxy, the two earlier aircraft still form the bulk of the service's cargo and tanker fleets and are expected to do so beyond the year 2000.

At the lower end of the scale, machines like the British Short's 330 and Spain's CASA 212 Aviocar are each making respectable inroads upon the virtually worldwide market for the smaller, twin-turboprop, rough field military transport.

Specialized support aircraft

The more specialized support aircraft are of relatively recent origin, stemming, in turn, from World War II development of airborne radar and related electronics equipment. Operationally, they can be grouped under two broad headings – surveillance and jamming.

Within the realms of surveillance, the E-3 Sentinel, Nimrod AEW3 and Grumman E-2 Hawkeye can all use their radar to peer out over a radius of around 200 miles from the parent aircraft. They can spot potential hostile activity beyond international borders, and direct the relevant friendly force's response.

Jamming enemy radar detection and radio communication links seems to call for ever more potent equipment, both in terms of the necessary specialized electronics and the aircraft to carry them. Both the US Navy and US Air Force put a great deal of emphasis on the ability of their forces of combat aircraft to penetrate enemy air space with the minimum chance of being detected. They have produced solutions to their problems in the shape of the EA-6B Prowler and the EF-111 – each of which carries an individual aircraft price tag well in excess of $35 million.

Right Northrop's latest export offering, the F-20 Tigershark, employs much of the F-5E's airframe, but has been re-engined around the single powerful General Electric F404 turbofan.

Far Right Two of a growing number of US Air Force operated F-5E Tigers.

Center The 'go-it-alone' British-developed Tornado F2 fighter variant of the joint Anglo-Federal German-Italian produced Panavia Tornado strike aircraft, 165 Tornado F2s are currently entering service with the Royal Air Force.

Left An F-5E Tiger of the Swiss Air Force rolls right against an Alpine backdrape. More than 2,750 F-5s have been built to date.

Above Northdrop's F-5F Tiger, the 2-seat variant of this widely exported twin General Electric J85-powered fighter.

Above Left To be replaced by the Tornado F2, the BAC Lightning F6 remains in service with West German-based Royal Air Force units.

Right This 11 Squadron Tornado GR1 two seat, twin engined low level strike aircraft is one of 220 GR1s being delivered to the Royal Air Force.

Right The shape of fighters to come? Grumman's X-29A forward swept wing research aircraft is being developed with US Air Force support to study design features for future combat aircraft.

Above General Dynamics F111E of the US Air Force.

Below A Panavia Tornado of the Federal German Navy's 1st Air Wing. 112 of these all-weather swing wing are slated for delivery to this navy.

Below The Soviet's Tu-96/142 'Bear' turboprop bomber's primary role is to direct cruise missiles at targets far beyond the visual or even radar range of the missile launcher, probably a warship.

Above Britain's first jet bomber, the English Electric Canberra is still operational with a number of air forces, this aircraft belonging to the Argentinian Air Force.

Upper Right The Douglas A-4M Skyhawk remains in front-line service with the US Marine Corps. First flown in June 1954, nearly 3,000 A-4s were built before production ended in early 1979.

Upper Left A tanker's eye view of Boeing B-52G, of which 193 were built. This bomber, along with the B-52H, can carry up to 20 AGM-86 air-launch cruise missiles, eight of which are carried internally with another twelve slung from beneath the two underwing pylons seen in this view.

Lower Right A French Air Force two-seat operational trainer version of the Jaguar.

Center Boeing's B-52H Stratofortress, the last of the line. In all, 102 of this model were built, the last being delivered to the US Air Force's Strategic Air Command in October 1962.

Lower Left This two-seat Douglas TA-4J Skyhawk is one of around 60 still employed with the US Navy for advanced pilot training.

Above A Royal Air Force
SEPECAT Jaguar GR1 single seat
strike variant of the collaborative
Anglo-French design.

Left A US Air Force/Air National
Guard Vought A-7D Corsair II.
This single-engined, single-
seater can loft up to 15,000 lbs of
bombs.

Upper Grumman's A-6E Intruder twin-engined, all-weather carrier aircraft has been the mainstay of the US Navy's bomber strength since the mid-1960s and continues in production today.

Center 64 of these Dassault Mirage IV supersonic bombers were build during the 1960s to spearhead France's man-delivered nuclear force.

Lower A characteristic in-flight study of the two-seat A-6E Intruder, showing the forward-mounted probe used for in-flight refueling.

Left Planview of the McDonnell AV-8B Harrier II now entering service with the US Marine Corps, who require more than 330 of these machines.

Above A Sea Harrier FR1 of the Royal Navy showing the machine's underside weapons to advantage.

Lower Left A British Aerospace Harrier GR3 of the Royal Air Force unleashing a salvo of underwing pod-mounted rockets.

Lower Right Two Sea Harrier FR1s of 801 Squadron Royal Navy, seen in the new post-Falklands color scheme.

Above and Below Two General Dynamics F111Ds of the US Air Force's Tactical Air Command. Despite serious early setbacks, this twin engined, swing wing machine is now one of the most effective low-level, all-weather strike aircraft.

Right This US Marine Corps' AV-8A Harrier is one of more than a hundred bought by the Marines. Spain also operates AV-8As.

Above Dassault's Super Etendard.

Far Left An AV-8B frontal aspect, showing its increased wing size compared with the earlier Harrier.

Above Left Lockheed's P-3C Orion long ranged, land-based maritime patrol aircraft has been in production for over 20 years and serves with the US Navy and numerous overseas countries.

Above The US Navy's carrier-based Lockheed S-3A Viking anti-submarine aircraft, of which over 180 were built.

Left Although long replaced in US Navy service by the S-3A Viking, Grumann's S-2 Tracker is still operational in some numbers in Australia, Argentina, Brazil and elsewhere around South America.

Above The Royal Air Force's
British Aerospace Nimrod MR2,
based on the De Havilland Comet
airliner airframe, ranges far out
to the north and west of Britain in
its mission to monitor Soviet Navy
surface ship and submarine
movements. Clearly visible are
the Sidewinder air-to-air missiles
added to give the aircraft some
self-defense capability.

Right Carrier deck view
of Dasault's Super Etendard.
Serving with the navies
ot France and Argentina, along
with the Iraqi Air Force, it was a
machine of this type that was
responsible for the loss of HMS
Sheffield and MS *Atlantic
Conveyor* during the Falklands
conflict of 1982.

Left France's latest maritime patrol aircraft, the Dassault-Breguet Atlantique 2, of which 42 are being built for the French Navy.

Above The Brazilian-developed EMBRAER EMB-111 is used for offshore patrol by the services of Brazil, Chile and Gabon.

Below This line up of the Swiss-developed Pilatus PC-7 Turbo Trainer belongs to the Royal Malaysian Air Force. More than 330 PC-7s have been sold to a dozen countries during the past six years.

Bottom The British Aerospace Hawk T1, standard advanced trainer employed by the Royal Air Force, can be armed with two Sidewinder missiles for airfield defense duties in times of crisis.

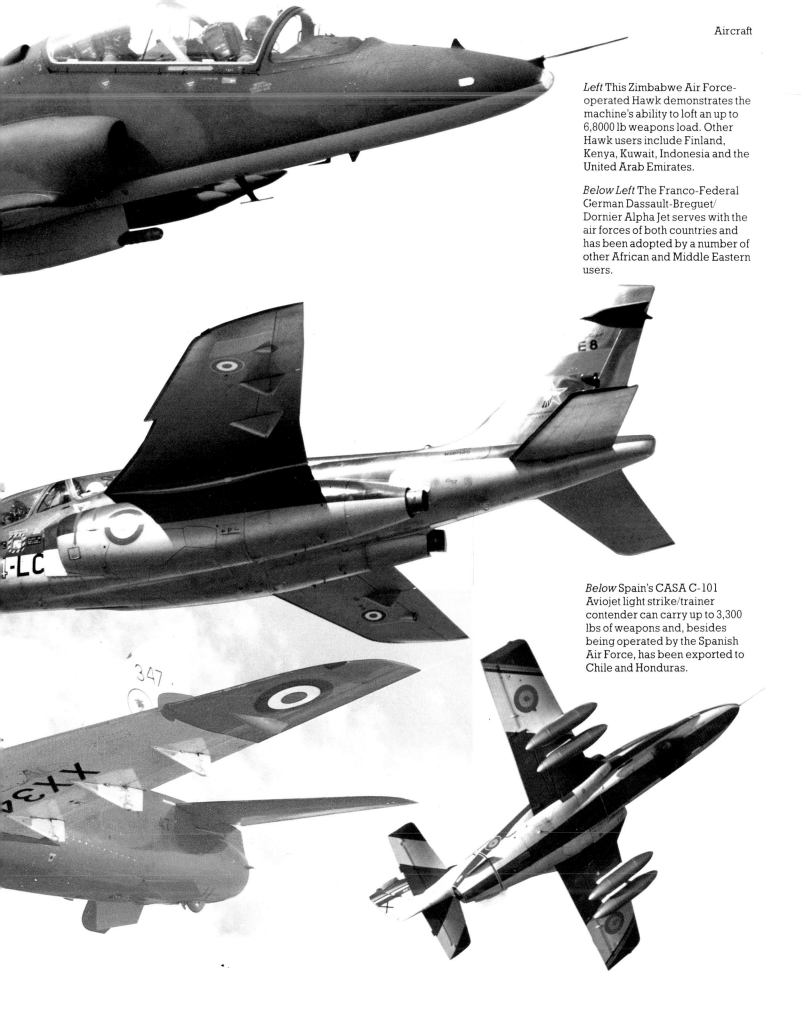

Left This Zimbabwe Air Force-operated Hawk demonstrates the machine's ability to loft an up to 6,8000 lb weapons load. Other Hawk users include Finland, Kenya, Kuwait, Indonesia and the United Arab Emirates.

Below Left The Franco-Federal German Dassault-Breguet/Dornier Alpha Jet serves with the air forces of both countries and has been adopted by a number of other African and Middle Eastern users.

Below Spain's CASA C-101 Aviojet light strike/trainer contender can carry up to 3,300 lbs of weapons and, besides being operated by the Spanish Air Force, has been exported to Chile and Honduras.

Above Signifying the growing
use of inflight refueling; a Royal
Air Force Victor BK2 tanker
transferring fuel to a Tornado.

Above The economic-to-operate
Fairchild Republic T-46A trainer
about to enter US Air Force
service as a Cessna T-37
replacement.

Center Capable of lofting nearly
a ton of weapons, Brazil's
EMBRAER EMB-312 Tucano is in
service with the Brazilian Air
Force and on order for Egypt and
Iraq, taking total orders to over
300.

Far Left The Scottish Aviation
Bulldog armed basic trainer
operates with a number of air
forces, including those of
Sweden, Kenya, Nigeria, Jordan.

Left The McDonnell Douglas T-45
carrier-going US Navy trainer, of
which around 350 will be
required, is, in fact, a variant of
the British Aerospace Hawk
strengthened for carrier
operation.

Right Grumman's ungainly E-2C
Hawkeye provides an airborne
early warning capability, plus the
means to control and direct
friendly aircraft to and from the
target.

Center Designed to fly bulky
cargo on and off US Navy aircraft
carriers, the Grumman C-2
Greyhound employs many
assemblies common to the E-2
Hawkeye.

Below Typical of the numerous
lighter military transports in use
around the world is this Brazilian
Air Force EMBRAER EMB-110.

Upper and Lower Right
Lockheed built 265 examples of their C-141A Starlifter, of which 271 were recently rebuilt and stretched to C-141B standard, as shown in the comparative view, while the close-up provides a useful idea of this 35 ton load carrier's size.

Right The US Navy's Grumman EA-6B Prowler carries over six tons of powerful electronic jamming equipment to cripple enemy radar and defense communication networks.

Above Another view of the Grumman E-2C Hawkeye, an aircraft deployed not only by the US Navy, but also by Japan and Israel.

Left The US Air Force's latest and largest tanker/cargo aircraft, the McDonnell Douglas KC-10A Extender, 60 of which are on order.

Top Right The US Air Force's massive Lockheed C-5A Galaxy, of which 81 were built, is shortly to be supplemented by a further 50 examples of the improved C-5B model.

Center The SIAI-Marchetti S.211, an Italian-developed design, aimed at the light jet strike-trainer markets of the Third World.

Left Boeing's KC-135A Stratotanker, for many years the backbone of the US Air Force's tanker fleet, is currently receiving a new lease of life as around 330 of them are relifed and re-engined.

Above Right The British Aerospace Nimrod AEW3 early warning and control aircraft now in service with the Royal Air Force is characterized by its relatively compact nose.

Below The Belfast, Northern Ireland-built Short 330, here seen in the colors of the Royal Thai Army. The US Air Force operates it as their C-23A Sherpa.

Right Boeing's E-3A Sentry carries a crew of four to fly the aircraft plus thirteen technicians to operate its airborne warning and control equipment.

Below Two of the 41 EMBRAER EMB-121 Xingu trainer/light transport bought for use by both the French Air Force and Navy.

Above The US Air Force's Boeing E-4B airborne command post is kept aloft as a last-ditch method of controlling the nation's military capability of retaliation.

Upper Right Following the US Navy's EA-6B example, Grumman have developed the EF-111A electronics jammer for the US Air Force, for whom over 40 existing F-111s are being converted.

HELICOPTERS

These Pages: US Army AH-IS
Huey Cobras.

Introduction

The emergence of the military helicopter as a vital element both in the conduct of a battle and in battle support and resupply is a fairly recent development. The helicopter as a concept, however, has been with us for over 500 years. It originated from the visionary pen of the multi-talented Italian, Leonardo Da Vinci, who, in 1483, drew up a scheme for a manpowered "Aerial Screw Machine". For the next four centuries, others, including Britain's Sir George Cayley in 1843, took up the challenge of producing a flying machine supported by rotating wings, but to little avail.

The first helicopters

It was only at the start of this century, when the fundamental problem of producing relatively lightweight, high power-to-weight engines had been solved, that the helicopter, became a practical proposition. Between the Breguet-Richet 4-rotor machine flown in September 1907 and the Spaniard Isacco's single powered rotor design of 1929, at least eight designs were flown with varying degrees of success. By June 1936, the known tally had risen to twelve, including the Focke Achgelis Fa-61, which was to take the world by storm.

Generally considered to be the world's first truly practical helicopter, the twin-rotored Fa-61 rapidly smashed all preceding helicopter records for speed, height and endurance by wide margins. By 1941, both the German Navy and the US Army were placing orders for the world's first two production helicopters, the Flettner Fl-282 Kolibri and Sikorsky R-4, respectively. The modern helicopter had emerged.

Enter the Helicopter

As in most sectors of aviation development of the latter 1930s, it was the Germans who played a major part in the shaping of the helicopter. This was true not only in a technical sense, but also in the molding of its mainstream roles.

In 1938, the German airline Lufthansa, impressed by the already proven performance of the Fa-61, agreed to sponsor the development of a scaled-up version that was to become the Fa-223 Drache. This, with its ability to lift a sling load of 2,000 lbs or four fully equipped troopers, was arguably the world's first production transport helicopter. At about the same time, another German, Anton Flettner, was developing a more compact family of helicopters, leading to the building of the ship-going Fl-282 Kolibri, designed to undertake anti-submarine duties. However, pressure for higher production of fixed wing aircraft, coupled with the ravages of World War II, resulted in only handfuls of machines ever actually entering operational service.

US developments

In America during the late 1930s the expatriate Russian, Igor Sikorsky, who had built his first helicopter in 1910, resurrected his interest in rotary-winged flight. Sikorsky began tethered flight trials with his VS-300 single rotor machine, followed by free flight testing of the aircraft in May 1940. Impressed by Sikorsky's efforts in this field, the US Army, who saw the helicopter's value as a rescue and communication vehicle, ordered his VS-316 design straight from the drawing board in late 1941. This helicopter, which was given the Army designation XR-4, flew for the first time in January 1942.

In all, 114 R-4s were to be built, many of which were transferred to the US Navy, Royal Air Force and Royal Navy for their evaluation. By August 1943, Sikorsky was flying his much more powerful S-51/R-5 design. This was the first of the truly mass-produced Sikorsky helicopters, built not only in the US but also by Westland in Britain, who produced a total of 183 license-built S-51s, mainly for Royal Air Force or Royal Navy use.

In 1942, another American, Lawrence Bell, turned his attention to the helicopter. Bell's painstaking work was to prove as fruitful as that of Sikorsky, leading to the renowned Model 47 design, which was first flown in December 1945. Under its US Army designation of H-13, the Bell Model 47 remains in worldwide military and civil use today.

Top Left Igor Sikorsky piloting his VS-300 during early tests in 1940.

Above Bell's Arthur Young carrying out tethered testing of a working model helicopter.

Below The Focke Achgelis Fa-61 of 1936. While by no means the first helicopter to fly, the Fa-61's performance and reliability totally eclipsed all earlier machines.

Center A US Army Bell H13E on casualty evacuation duties in Korea. This machine is featured in the television series M.A.S.H.

Left A Piasecki H-21C of the French Air Force, who made extensive use of the type both in Indo-China and Algeria.

Below A line-astern formation of British Army Westland Lynx AH1s.

Left One of the 130 British Army operated Bell Model 47s, all of which were license-built by either Agusta or Westland.

Post-war development

The year 1947 marked the first major milestone in Britain's home-based helicopter development, with the first flights of the relatively conventional Bristol Sycamore and the less conventional Fairey Gyrodyne.

The Sycamore, which was followed in 1952 by the much larger, tandem-rotored Bristol Belvedere transport helicopter, was the first British helicopter to enter into widespread British service use. The Fairey Gyrodyne evolved by stages into the record-setting, 40-passenger Fairey Rotodyne, in which the Royal Air Force showed a keen interest even before its first flight in November 1957. The Rotodyne development, however, was shelved in 1962, mainly because of governmental policy shifts rather than for any technical reason. Four years earlier, the government had decided that all home-based British helicopter development being undertaken by Bristol, Fairey and Saunders-Roe should be placed in the hands of Westland Helicopter.

French efforts to develop a helicopter industry began in the early 1950s, leading to the Sud-Ouest SO 1220 Djinn light observation type, first flown in January 1953. The Djinn was followed just over two years later by the first flight of the larger Sud-Ouest SO 3130 Alouette light utility type, of which well over 1,300 examples were eventually built.

The only other country involved in helicopter development during the latter 1940s and early 1950s was the Soviet Union, whose Yakolev Yak-24 'Horse', a large, tandem-rotored transport machine, made its maiden flight in July 1953.

Vertical Infantry

In common with most other aspects of military development, the helicopter's evolution flourished particularly during the 1950s and 1960s. This was largely due to the impetus provided by a series of ongoing wars, from Korea and Malaysia at the start of the period, through Indo-China and Algeria, to the Middle East and Vietnam in later years.

US troops or US-built helicopters took part in all of these campaigns, with the exception of the British action in Malaysia. Consequently it was the American military helicopter and its supporting industry that was to reap the major benefits. The US Army, too, as purchaser, operator and future requirement specifier, played a crucial role in the overall scheme of things.

Left A Piasecki (now Boeing Vertol) H-25 Retriever of the US Air Force. Several hundred of this type were built for the US Navy/Marines, Army and Air Force, along with the services of Canada and France.

Center Bottom A US Air Force Sikorsky H-5D, specifically used on search and rescue duties.

Above A float-equipped Piasecki (now Boeing Vertol) H-21A Workhorse employed in the search and rescue role by the US Air Force.

Far Left Britain's first home-developed production helicopter, the Bristol Sycamore, was operated by both the Royal Air Force and British Army as well as by Belgium, Federal Germany and Australia. In all, 178 Sycamores were built.

Right The tandem-rotored Bristol Belvedere HC1, the Royal Air Force's first sizable transport helicopter.

Below Although never put into production, the sole US Air Force funded Hughes XH-17 pointed the way towards the truly massive flying crane loadlifter.

Far Right This US Army CH-47D Chinook is one of more than 900 so far delivered to numerous services worldwide since 1962.

Center Right A Sikorsky H-19A of the US Air Force. Variants of this 12-seat utility helicopter were used by all three US air arms, plus many overseas armed services.

Far Right The US Army made much use of the 12 troop-carrying Bell UH-1D in Vietnam, often operated, as here, in sufficiently large numbers to airlift more than a thousand infantry rapidly in or out of the battle area.

Bottom Right While far less ambitious than the Hughes XH-17, Sikorsky's S-56 could still lift sizable loads, including internally-carried light vehicles. Operated by the US Marines as the HR2S and by the US Army as the CH-37A Mojave, a total of 154 were built.

The needs of the US Army

In 1947, the US Army had its air force element decoupled from it. From then until the early 1950s the newly formed US Air Force was allowed to lead in terms of helicopter development. From the Army's viewpoint, this was a rather unsatisfactory period during which, largely by Air Force default, the US Navy were increasingly allowed to dictate the kind of helicopters being drawn up by Sikorsky, Bell and Piasecki (now Boeing Vertol). Realizing this, the US Army started to push their own requirements, commencing in 1955, when they issued the specification that gave birth to the 12-troop carrying Bell Model 204/205/212 family, perhaps better known as the UH-1 series.

In 1959, the Army ordered its first large assault type in the shape of the Boeing Vertol CH-47 Chinook, completing a four-card trick with its 1962 specifications for a light scouting helicopter and an armed and armored gunship; needs that led directly to the Hughes OH-6 Cayuse and Bell AH-1 Hueycobra respectively. By the mid-1960s, when the US was becoming more and more involved in South East Asia, its Army was in a position to provide all of the various mission types required to transport, land and support its fighting troops along tactical lines devised during the 1960s.

Only the Soviet Union has been able, even in part, to match the development of the US battlefield helicopter. The Soviets have tended to concentrate their efforts around the development of even larger sized assault and transport helicopters, plus formidable gunships in the shape of the Mil-24 'Hind'. In general, the pace of Soviet military helicopter development has lagged somewhat behind that of the US – the Soviets have yet to produce a machine comparable to the Bell UH-1.

Today, with its large number of rebuilt CH-47 Chinooks, backed by the smaller Sikorsky UH-60A Black Hawk and Hughes AH-64 Apache gunships coming into service, the US Army looks set to maintain its dominant influence on the battlefield helicopter and its use.

Right A Chinook HC1 of the Royal Air Force lifting a Scorpion light tank.

Below A US Army Boeing Vertol CH-47D Chinook demonstrating its battlefield usefulness by airlifting in a heavy field howitzer.

Bottom Right Prior to the 1979 Iranian Revolution, Iran placed a series of large orders for the Bell Model 214, a development of the UH-1, of which 335 had been handed over when deliveries were halted.

The Helicopter Goes to Sea

1985 marks the 21st anniversary of the Royal Navy's first operational deployment of the anti-submarine torpedo-carrying Westland Wasp, from the decks of its Tribal class frigates. This event, along with the Royal Canadian Navy's slightly later deployment of the larger Sikorsky SH-3 Sea King, began the era of the modern, small-ship-going anti-submarine helicopter, now taken for granted by navies throughout the world.

Much of the early post-World War II naval helicopter development effort was led by the US Navy, who in conjunction with Sikorsky and Bell, evolved an ever-more effective series of anti-submarine types. These included the 1953 Bell HSL-1, the 1954 Sikorsky S-58/HSS and the 1959 Sikorsky S-61/SH-3 Sea King. The one drawback to these US Navy developments was that none of these aircraft could operate on anything smaller than an aircraft carrier or a large, clear-decked transport ship.

As to the British and Canadian development work on the small-ship-going helicopter, each service chose a fundamentally different approach. In the case of the British, the Wasp represented about the smallest machine capable of lifting two men and two lightweight torpedoes. It made minimal demands on the parent ship, necessitating only the addition of a light hangar, topped by a fold-down landing platform or helipad. In contrast, to operate the Sea King, the Canadians had virtually to redesign their frigate fleet. Around fifty per cent of the upper deck area had to be given over to the hangarage and helipad needed to accommodate a single Sea King.

Saving space

Most of the world's navies have adopted the British approach of attempting to minimize the amount of ship weight and space devoted to helicopter operations and stowage. (Only the Japanese have elected to follow the Canadian pattern.) One of the best examples is the Italian-developed Esmeraldas class corvette of only 700 tons full displacement, which, while lacking a hangar, has an elevated helipad large enough to operate an Agusta-Bell AB 212ASW helicopter.

Today, there are approximately 1,200 small ship-going naval helicopters, ranging from the high capability/high cost Sikorsky SH-60B Seahawk and Westland Lynx, through the French-developed Aerospatiale AS 365 Dauphin II, to the less expensive, if more operationally limited, Hughes Models 500D ASW and MBB Bo-105. Of these, nearly 150 now carry a useful secondary anti-ship strike capability, made possible by recent development in compacting the size of the missile and its associated electronics.

Below Center The role versatility of the military helicopter is demonstrated by this US Army UH-1D equipped with outrigger mine dispensers, each capable of laying a track of up to 70 anti-tank or anti-personnel mini-mines.

Below Closeup of the Royal Air Force's transport helicopter, the Bristol Belvedere HC1.

The Tank Killers

During the early 1960s the US Army Bell AH-1 Huey Cobra emerged, leading the world into the development of the armed and armored gunship helicopter. As originally designed, the AH-1 was a single engined machine but in later models it appeared, with US Marine Corps support, as a twin-engined helicopter, providing a higher degree of crew safety from battle damage. Over the years, the AH-1 family has grown not only in its total installed power, but also in the range and weight of weaponry that can be hung from it, including cannon, rockets and ever more potent anti-tank missiles. Today's US Army's Hughes AH-64 Apache can carry up to sixteen long-range Hellfire anti-tank missiles, plus 1,200 rounds of 30mm ammunition. Benefiting from the massive bank of US Army gunship operating experience, it can both hand out and tolerate more combat punishment than any previous helicopter.

Escalating costs

The cost of developing machines such as the AH-64, when all research costs are recovered over the current 515 aircraft program, runs at around $13 million each. Obviously, few services outside of those of the world's leading nations could afford such a machine. However, advances in the fields of anti-tank missiles and electronics in recent years have brought the tank-killing helicopter within the reach of the less affluent armies of the world.

With the development of 'off-the-shelf' weaponry and the associated aiming equipment, it is now possible to buy a virtually standard commercial helicopter, strap on the additional military hardware and be ready to go into the tank-killing business. However, this alternative buys a limited operational capability and an aircraft with a very low tolerance even to light enemy ground fire. Despite these dangers, there are today numerous armies operating just such light armed helicopters, which, so long as they maintain an element of surprise, can still inflict a considerable mauling on an advancing enemy armored ground force. Interestingly, a number of European helicopter manufacturers are developing anti-armor gunships of their own, such as Italy's Agusta A129 Mangusta and the joint Franco-German PAH-2, both of which are aimed at costing less than the top-of-the-market AH-64.

Right and Far Right The French-developed Aerospatiale SA 330 H/L Puma medium-sized transport helicopter has been a valuable export earner with sales to around 25 overseas countries, plus the 48 SA 330C models built for the Royal Air Force. Including French-operated Pumas, more than 600 have been sold, of which the vast majority are for military use.

Above The US Marine Corps
made large-scale use of the Bell
UH-1 in their South East Asian
operations, this pair being UH-
1Es.

Into the Future

The military and naval helicopter has provided greater freedom to deploy and support forces on land or at sea than was once even dreamed of. Yet helicopters have their drawbacks. They are slow compared with fixed-winged aircraft, and their operating and maintenance costs are higher than those of a fixed-winged machine capable of lifting the same load.

Because of the helicopter's complex and crucial rotating lift and control producing rotor systems, its parts require more frequent inspection, and in some cases, replacement, than on a comparable fixed-wing aircraft. These aspects are part and parcel of the helicopter's makeup, and rotary-winged users have, on the whole, learned to live with them. It is true that the complexity of helicopter rotor and power transmission systems have been simplified somewhat over the years, but progress on these fronts is slow.

Limited top speed

The helicopter's limited top speed is also fundamental, for while it continues to rely on a rotating lift system, its rotor-tip speeds can encounter all the problems associated with transonic flight even when the aircraft itself is flying at a modest forward speed. Indeed, while a few specially designed or modified military helicopters have exceeded speeds of 200 mph, the vast majority have top speeds in the range between 125 mph to 160 mph. Even so, there are ways to overcome the helicopter's limited forward speed problem. One solution is to provide the machine with wings and forward thrusting motive power, as in the case of the early 1930s autogyros.

More recently, helicopter designers, particularly in the US, have turned their attention to incorporating some form of main rotor system that will enable the machine to rise vertically under the thrust of rotation, after which the specially shaped rotor is stopped in such a position as to provide the same lift characteristics as those of a normal aircraft wing (as in the US-developed X-wing concept).

Another approach to the problem currently being studied in the US is that of tilting the machine's engines and rotors. This is the principle behind the joint Boeing-Bell JVX design. With all of this research going on, there is a distinct possibility that the 300 mph-plus, half-helicopter-half-airplane is just around the corner.

Upper Right The US Air Force's Sikorsky HH-60D Night Hawk is a specialized, all-weather search and rescue variant of the US Army's UH-60A Black Hawk.

Upper Left and Lower Right The Sikorsky UH-60A Black Hawk has now largely replaced the Bell UH-1 as the US Army's prime squad-sized troop transport. UH-60As first saw action in Grenada during early 1984.

Lower Left The Hughes Model 500 MD Defender, carries four TOIV anti-tank missiles.

Above One of 30 Dutch Army operated MBB Bo-105s. More than 220 military models have been exported to or license-built in countries as far afield as Spain and Indonesia.

Right Another shot of the Sikorsky UH-60A Black Hawk in action.

Above Sikorsky's SH-3 Sea King, developed specifically for the US Navy, represented a major breakthrough in anti-submarine helicopter capability and will remain in widespread service into the next century, some forty years after its operational debut.

Left A HOT anti-tank missile equipped MBB Bo-105 of the Federal German Army, who operate more than 200 Bo-105s.

Left A Westland Commando of the Egyptian Air Force. The Commando is an anglicized development of Sikorsky's S.61/SH-3 Sea King.

Left Inset Still in service with the British Army after more than 21 years is Westland's turbo shaft-powered and highly respected Scout AH1.

Above The Aerospatiale SA 330 H/L Puma medium-sized transport helicopter.

Left A Royal Navy Westland-Sikorsky Sea King HAS 5. Westland have been particularly successful in selling the machine to overseas users.

Below Left An Agusta license-built SH-3D Sea King of the Italian Navy. While Sikorsky no longer produce the type it remains in production in both Britain and Italy.

Below Right The Sikorsky SH-60B Seahawk, seen here in prototype form, represents the current generation of US Navy sub-killers.

Right Sikorsky's SH-60B Seahawk shipboard sub-killer, recently introduced into US Navy service, is a derivative of the UH-60A Black Hawk.

Below A US Navy SH-60B Seahawk operating over San Diego. Original plans called for the purchase of 204 Seahawks, but this number may be increased.

Above The US Navy's Sikorsky HSS-1/SH-34 Seabat, put into service in 1955, is generally considered to be the first effective sub-killer.

Above Sea King, Wessex 1 and Gazelle helicopters.

Left A Westland-Sikorsky Sea King HAS 2 hastily fitted with long range search radar for deployment with Britain's Falklands garrison forces.

Below This US Navy Kaman NHH-2D is seen carrying out early shipboard-going trials aboard the Belknap class cruiser USS Fox (CG 38).

Right A US Navy 31 Helicopter Squadron Kaman SH-2F Seasprite coming in to land aboard the aft helicopter platform of a Knox class frigate. The Seasprite still provides the bulk of the US Navy small ship sub-killing capability.

Below Sikorsky's CH-53E Super Stallion provides the US Marine Corps with a massive airborne heavy assault capability, with more than 140 planned for delivery to the service by 1992, plus models for the US Navy.

Left The Sikorsky MH-53E Super Stallion will shortly enter the US Navy as an aerial minesweeper, supplementing and ultimately replacing the fleet of earlier MH-53D machines currently employed on these duties.

Above The Soviet Navy's Kamov Ka-25 'Hormone' still provides the bulk of Russia's ship-going anti-submarine and anti-ship targeting capability.

Upper Left The US Navy still operates a large number of Bel UH-1Ns on inter-ship utility and communications duties.

Lower Left A French Navy Aerospatiale SA321G Super Frelon, seen here armed with the ship-killing Exocet missile.

Above Two US Marine Corps' CH-53E Super Stallions refuel in flight from a US Navy Lockheed KC-130H Hercules tanker.

Right The Hughes Model 500 MD ASW represents about the most compact sub-killing helicopter available. A number of these small ship-going machines have been sold to Far Eastern navies.

Left An Italian Navy Agusta-Bell AB212ASW sub-killer. Developed in Italy from the Bell UH-1N, more than 100 AB212ASWs have been sold to a number of navies around the world.

Below A Westland Lynx HAS2
going aboard the Royal Navy
Leander class frigate HMS *Danae*
(F47). Around 200 naval Lynx
have been sold.

Below Right The US Marine
Corps employs the Bell AH-1T
gunship in support of amphibious
troop landings from US Navy
assault ships, such as their
Tarawa class vessels.

Far Left One of the early US Marine Corps' Bell AH-1Js showing its ability to operate from a US Navy frigate's helipad.

Center Left The joint Anglo-Italian European Helicopter Industries EH-101, seen here in Italian Navy colors, is scheduled to enter service during the 1980s as a Sea King replacement with both countries.

Left The Mil-4 'Hound' was the Soviet Navy's first sub-killer, but was always operated from land bases. A few remain in service with a number of Eastern Bloc navies, including that of mainland China.

Below All US Navy helicopter pilots have to start somewhere and, currently, it is the Bell TH-57A that provides their basic training.

Above A Royal Navy Westland Lynx HAS2 equipped with four Sea Skua anti-ship missiles; a combination that proved highly effective during the 1982 Falkland Islands campaign.

Right Simply keeping a shipboard helicopter aboard can present problems as can be seen with this Lynx HAS2 aboard the Royal Navy destroyer HMS *Birmingham* (D86).

Top Right Still in widespread naval service today, the Westland Wasp became the world's first small ship-going sub-killer when it was first deployed aboard Royal Navy Tribal class frigates in 1965.

Center Right This French Navy-operated Lynx HAS2, here seen aboard the destroyer *Georges Leygues* (D640), is one of 40 delivered. The Georges Leygues class ships each carry two Lynx.

Above Crew members of a Mexican Navy Uribe class patrol vessel manhandle the ship's MBB Bo-105 ASW into the maindeck hangar.

Left The Aerospatiale SA319B Alouette III is operated with a number of navies, including that of France, shown here, who retain the type for anti-submarine helicopter crew training.

Right Despite the advent of the AH-64A Apache, the US Army's Bell AH-1S HueyCobra will remain in front-line service for many years yet, thanks to a major programme of airframe relifing and equipment modernization.

Below Although primarily operated as a Royal Navy training|type, these Westland-built Aerospatiale SA341 Gazelle HT2s can double as light communications helicopters, several serving in this role from Royal Navy ships taking part in the Falklands Islands conflict.

Above The Federal German Army's MBB Bo-105/PAH-1 tank-killer.

Left France's Aerospatiale SA341L, seen here cannon equipped, not only serves with the French Army, but has exported in large numbers to many overseas military air arms.

Below This British Army Westland Lynx AH1 is capable of carrying up to eight TOW anti-tank missiles. Around 120 military Lynx have been sold to date.

Above Iran operates the Bell AH-1J HueyCobra, 202 being delivered prior to the 1979 Iranian Revolution. Around 60 can carry four TOW anti-tank missiles.

Right Many of the US Army's Bell AH-1Gs, seen here, have been rebuilt to AH-1S standard.

Below Right A trio of US Army Bell AH-1 gunships operating over Vietnam. In all, around 2,000 AH-1s of all models have been built by Bell.

Below The formidable Soviet Mil-24 'Hind' gunship has played a major role in countering Muslim partisans in Afghanistan.

Above Two US Marine Corps' Bell AH-1T Sea Cobras.

Left The Federal German Army's MBB Bo-105/PAH-1 tank-killer, equipped to carry six HOT anti-tank missiles.

Below A Westland Lynx AH1 of the British Army unleashing a salvo of anti-armor rocket projectiles.

Above and Left The US Army's latest tank-killer, the Hughes AH-64A Apache can operate in all weathers and carries up to 16 long range Hellfire anti-tank missiles as well as over 1,200 rounds of 30mm ammunition for its rapid-fire, electronically directed cannon.

115

Left and Bottom Right A TOIV anti-tank missile-equipped Hughes Model 500MD Defender.

Right and Below The Agusta A109, which, like the MBB Bo-105, started life as a commercial helicopter, has been bought by the armies of Argentina, Libya and Yugoslavia for anti-armor missions. More lately, Augusta have developed the more heavily armed and armored A129 Mangusta, on order for the Italian Army.

Above and Left Two informative views of Sikorsky's militarized AUH-76 version of their S-76 MkII commercial machine. Ordered by the Philippines, the anti-armor AUH-76 can carry up to 16 TOW missiles, or 12 troops when operating as a utility transport.

Above and Bottom Right
Sikorsky have amassed much
flying experience on their
Advancing Blade Concept (ABC)
XH-59A, dating back to 1973.

Below Sikorsky have built this
prototype helicopter specifically
to gain in-flight experience with
new lightweight material and
construction techniques.

Left and Right The Sikorsky S-72 experimental airplane-cum-helicopter has been flown with and without wings and recently without rotors.

Top Right A proposed Hughes Helicopters design for a light fast scouting helicopter.

TANKS

Tank and crew at rest during a
lull in fighting in the Middle East.

Introduction

Just under seventy years ago, after the outbreak of World War I, the tank made its first appearance on the battlefield. Its role was to break the deadlock of trench warfare in France, brought about by the advent of the machine gun, the magazine rifle and the quick-firing artillery gun. The first tanks did not succeed; they were too primitive in design. However, by the end of World War I, in November 1918, the potential of the tank had already been realized.

The era of Blitzkrieg

During the next twenty years many nations experimented with tanks, but it was only the Germans who really appreciated the effect that they could have, if properly handled. The result was their Blitzkrieg or 'lightning war' campaigns of 1939-42, which changed the face of Europe.

The Allies soon learnt the lesson, and the tank dominated all theaters of World War II, apart from the jungles of the Pacific Islands and Burma. Both sides soon realized that, for the tank to be decisive on the battlefield, it needed help from other sections of the army, especially the infantry and artillery. Yet these had to be able to keep up with the tank, and hence other types of armored fighting vehicle were quickly developed, including Infantry Combat Vehicles and self-propelled artillery.

Modern warfare

Since 1945 armored vehicles have remained a cornerstone of national armories, and there have been few conflicts in which they have not made an appearance. They have fought in major wars such as those between Israel and the Arab States, and in Vietnam; and they have equally served in counter-insurgency operations in places as far afield as Northern Ireland and Afghanistan.

New threats to the tank have been developed, especially the anti-tank guided missile, used by infantry in the 1973 Yom Kippur War, or mounted in helicopters, as used against North Vietnamese armor in 1972. These have caused some people to conclude that the day of the tank is almost over. This is not so: the tank is still as dominant as ever, particularly in Europe. If World War III should ever come, it would be mainly fought on land. The Soviets rely very heavily on armor to achieve quick victory, while the West places just as much emphasis on it in order to deny this to the Soviets.

The tank on its own, however, is not a decisive weapon in any battle. There are many different types of armored vehicle, and it is these operating together in the right mix, along with other weapon systems, which produce the recipe for victory in the land battle.

Master Weapon of War

The tank is essentially a mobile gun platform, whose tasks on the battlefield are the destruction of enemy armored vehicles, providing close support to friendly infantry and above all – shock action – the ability to hit the enemy hard at the critical moment in battle.

Devastating firepower

For shock action, firepower is all-important. Over the years tank guns have increased in size and the most popular is now the 120mm caliber tank gun. Today's tanks can hit enemy armored vehicles and destroy them out to ranges of over 3000 yards.

Up until recently the barrel was always rifled (lined with a spiral groove). This gave maximum accuracy by imparting spin to the projectile. Now, however, many nations have adopted the smoothbore gun. This enables hotter charges to be used, which will send the projectile further, and the problem of accuracy has been overcome by giving the projectile fins so that it flies through the air like a dart.

Modern shells

The tank gun uses two types of ammunition: Kinetic Energy ammunition, which relies on speed and mass to penetrate armor, and Chemical Energy ammunition, where the chemical effect when it hits the target is what counts most. Kinetic Energy projectiles are made of very hard metal. The thicker or more sloped the armor, the less chance they have to penetrate.

With Chemical Energy rounds, it does not matter how thick or sloped the armor is. One type is called High Explosive Squashhead. This has a soft metal nose, is filled with explosive and has a base fuze. When it hits an enemy tank it 'cowpats' on the armor and the fuze detonates the explosive. This sends shock waves through the armor, causing pieces of it to break off on the inside and fly around the turrret and hull.

The other type of Chemical Energy round is the High Explosive Anti-tank or Hollow Charge round. This has an inverted cone-shaped hollow in the front, lined with metal, and explosive in the rear. When it hits the target it detonates and sends a thin jet of molten metal through the armor.

To guard against Chemical Energy attack, spaced armor – two thicknesses of armor with a space in between – and laminated armor, made up of a sandwich of different materials, are used. Hollow Charge warheads are also used in anti-tank guided missiles.

Left Chieftain, which has been in British service since 1967 and is likely to continue to be so for a number of years. This one is mounting simulated firing equipment for use in training and the orange smoke indicates that it has been hit.

Far Left The Soviet T-80. This is essentially a T-72, but with an improved fire control system and better armor.

Ten seconds to strike

To be effective, the tank has to identify and destroy its target quickly. The equipment used to spot the target and lay the gun accurately on it is called the fire control system. Nowadays, this is very sophisticated and is made up of the commander's and gunner's sights, a laser rangefinder and a computer. The computer plots the path of the projectile through the air, and tells the gunner which part of his sight to lay on the target. This gives him a very good chance of spotting and hitting an enemy tank all within ten seconds. The crew also have special sights for use by night and so the tank is able to fight 'round the clock'.

The main battle tank of today weighs 50-60 tons and has a very powerful engine, enabling it to travel at speeds of up to 40 mph. Diesel engines are now used instead of gas engines because they are less likely to catch fire, and they have a better fuel consumption. Even so, a modern tank has a range of little more than 200 miles on maximum fuel, or less if it is doing much cross-country work. Tanks use automatic gearboxes, and with several reverse gears, can travel as fast backwards as they can forwards. This is very important if a tank is caught in the open and wants to get behind cover quickly.

Fighting crew

Most tanks have a crew of four. In the turret are the commander, who is in charge, the gunner and the loader, who also operates the radios. The driver is the one member in the hull. Some tanks, however, especially Soviet ones, have replaced the loader by a machine, the autoloader, which means that the turret does not have to be so large. The crew will normally fight from inside the tank with the hatches closed, especially if there is a threat of chemical or nuclear weapons being used. The interior can be sealed and pure air passed through a filter, which is normally mounted at the rear of the turret.

Above The newest US tank is the M1 Abrams. The early model mounts the 105mm rifled gun, but later ones will have a 120mm smoothbore.

Above Center A Soviet T-54 tank. This was the main Soviet tank of the 1950s, but is still in service, although its 100mm rifled gun is little match for modern main battle tanks.

Right The Swedish Strv 103 or S Tank. Unlike other main battle tanks, it has no turret and has to turn on its tracks to traverse the gun.

Above Right Note how the gun barrel on this Chieftain has been camouflaged to break up its outline.

Below US M60 in winter conditions.

Eyes and Ears of the Army

No commander can expect to fight a battle and win it unless he has a good idea of what the enemy are doing. In this age of satellites and spy planes, it is easy to forget that there is still a very real need for effective reconnaissance on the ground, and much of this is provided by the armored reconnaissance vehicle.

The armored reconnaissance vehicle

There are two types of reconnaissance. Reconnaissance by fire is firing at the enemy position to persuade him to shoot back, thus giving away details of his position and equipment. The danger with this is that the reconnaissance vehicle might be destroyed before it can send back the information it has gained, and hence reconnaissance by stealth is preferred. This means getting into a position where the enemy can be seen, but cannot spot the

reconnaissance vehicle. To do this, the vehicle must be small, and can be propelled by wheels or tracks.

Wheeled vehicles have two major advantages over tracked ones. They are much quieter and are easier to maintain. They are also cheaper to produce. Tracked vehicles, however, have a much better cross-country performance and can traverse terrain which is impossible for a wheeled vehicle.

Guns for the job

If the reconnaissance vehicle is to see without being seen, there is a good argument for making it very lightly armed, with just a machine gun, for this helps to keep its overall size small. Yet there are times when it will be forced to fight for information, and a machine gun is of little use when confronted with another armored vehicle.

Left M551 Sheridan firing the Shillelagh missile.

Below Left Tanks require much maintenance to keep them fit for battle. Here a Chieftain gets a new power pack.

129

Right The crew of a US M551 Sheridan mount up. Designed as a reconnaissance tank, it is unique in that its 152mm gun fires both the Shillelagh anti-tank guided missile and a conventional HEAT round.

Far Right The US M60A1, mounting a dozer blade, which is used for improving fire positions, on exercise in Germany. This mounts a 105mm rifled gun, and is gradually being replaced by the M1 Abrams.

Right A West German Leopard 2 firing on the range.

Top Right US M1 Abrams on an approach march somewhere in Germany. Note how the crew's equipment is strapped onto the turret.

Some designers therefore opt for a 20-30mm cannon, which is effective against light armored vehicles, but not so against main battle tanks. Others argue that a reconnaissance vehicle should be able to engage a tank if necessary, and have a gun with caliber ranging from 76–105mm, or an anti-tank guided weapon system.

Endurance is all

Vehicle size also dictates the number of crewmen a reconnaissance car can carry. The minimum is two, one to drive and the other to command and observe. This keeps the vehicle small, but can be very tiring for the crew, who will often have to operate for days at a time without any rest. Many reconnaissance vehicles therefore have a crew of three — commander, gunner and driver — or if reconnaissance troops are also expected to perform tasks such as preparing booby traps or laying mines, there may be as many as five crewmen.

Instruments of vision

The reconnaissance vehicle's surveillance aids are its most important asset. In their simplest form these are the eyes and ears of the crew members. From a static position, the crew will often dismount, leave their vehicle behind cover and set up an observation post, running a telephone cable back to the vehicle radios.

A reconnaissance car is equipped with sights like those on a tank, with very good magnification; and its crew are able to see at night or in poor visibility, using infra-red or image intensification techniques. Some vehicles also mount radars, or have specialist devices to monitor nuclear radiation or the presence of chemical agents. The reconnaissance vehicle must be tailored to carry out its task but, in the event, it will only ever be as good as its crew.

Right A British Challenger undergoing mobility tests.

Far Right Chieftains night firing. They use infrared searchlights to identify their targets.

Right A fine shot of a Chieftain. Its 120mm rifled gun is still one of the most powerful in the world, and is used in Challenger.

Carrying the Infantry

On the mechanized battlefield of today infantry and tanks work very closely with one another. The infantryman must therefore be able to keep up with armor, and hence needs armored vehicles to carry him. For this, he has two types of specially designed vehicles: the Armored Personnel Carrier and the Mechanized Infantry Combat Vehicle (or Infantry Fighting Vehicle).

Battlefield transport

To the infantryman on the battlefield, the Armored Personnel Carrier is like a cab. It takes him to where he wants to go, drops him off, and then goes to the rear and waits for him to call for it again. In the attack it will take him close to his objective before he dismounts and sometimes, if the opposition is weak, will take him right into it, increasing the speed and momentum of the attack. It is also the infantryman's mobile home where he can store any equipment not in use at that time.

Each Armored Personnel Carrier can carry a squad of infantry — six to nine men — of whom the commander and the driver remain permanently with the vehicle. It is normally armed with just a machine gun, but some models also have weapons slits in the side of the hull to fire through.

Its protective armor is not as tough as that of a main battle tank, being designed merely to keep out shell splinters and small arms fire. Some models of Armored Personnel Carrier have collective nuclear and chemical protection in the same way as a tank, but others do not.

Sometimes the basic carrier is adapted to carry the infantryman's heavier weapons. Thus there are mortar carriers, from which a mortar can be fired through the roof hatch; recoilless anti-tank gun carriers; and anti-tank guided weapons carriers.

A mobile fortress

The Infantry Fighting Vehicle is, as its name suggests, a vehicle from which to fight. It has a turret with either a 20–30mm cannon or sometimes a medium caliber gun and sometimes anti-tank guided weapons systems as well. This armament is designed to engage light armored vehicles rather than main battle tanks: heavy tanks alongside are normally assigned to tackle enemy tanks.

The vehicle is also a personnel carrier, which, because it is a fighting vehicle, will remain much closer to the infantry when they have dismounted. But it must not stand too close beside them, for it may be seen and could draw artillery fire. It is therefore usually deployed some distance to one side. In terms of protection, the Infantry Fighting Vehicle has the same strength of armor as the personnel carrier.

Wheels or tracks?

Most Armored Personnel Carriers and Infantry Fighting Vehicles are tracked. However, wheeled infantry armored vehicles are much better suited to internal security roles, such as riot control. Internal security versions are often fitted with special-to-role items such as water cannon; fenders to ward off petrol bomb attacks; and plows for clearing consolidated roadblocks.

Two inherent dangers

The infantry's armored vehicles enable infantrymen to continue to play a major role in the land battle of today by giving them the ability to move about the battlefield under fire. In some ways, however, these vehicles have made the infantry a more recognizable target than they were before. Furthermore, the more heavily armed the vehicle, the more infantrymen have to stay on board as members of the permanent crew, and the fewer there will be to jump out of the back and carry out their vital dismounted tasks.

Modern Artillery

Without artillery to lay down quick and accurate supporting fire battles could not be won. Traditionally, artillery guns have always been mounted on wheels, drawn at first by horses and later by wheeled vehicles. Although this 'towed' artillery still exists, it is now normally deployed in more difficult terrain, such as jungle, mountains and marsh. There is, however, little place for it on today's fast-moving mechanized battlefield. Not only is it too vulnerable to enemy fire but, like the infantry, it needs to be able to keep up with the tank. Hence, modern artillery has been put on tracks, given some armor protection and the means to propel itself without the help of a towing vehicle.

Long-range fire

The essential difference between a tank and a self-propelled artillery gun is that of role. While tanks are designed to engage other armored vehicles that they can see to aim at (this is called

Right This Mowag 4-wheel variant is called Spy and mounts a 12.7mm machine gun.

Upper Right Many countries use the US Commando, which appears in a number of configurations. This V-150 version has twin 7.62mm machine guns and can carry up to 12 men.

Below The Swiss Mowag Shark firing its 105mm gun. There are also 4 and 6 wheel variants, some of which are used by the Canadian Army and US Marine Corps.

Left The latest US
reconnaissance vehicle – M3
Bradley, with a crew of five,
25mm cannon and guided missile
launchers.

Right British 76mm Scorpion tracked reconnaissance vehicle in the Arabian desert.

Bottom Right The Israeli Merkava, designed after much desert tank fighting experience. It is unusual in having the engine in the front, and a stowage compartment in the rear for extra ammunition or for carrying infantry.

direct fire), artillery fires at targets at up to ten times the range of a tank, and ones which the gun crew cannot see themselves.

To do this, the artillery crew relies on a forward observer to give the necessary target details and to direct the aim of fire. The term for this is indirect fire, and it is designed to lay down a heavy concentration of explosive over an area rather than a point target. For this, the artillery gun requires different sighting devices and a much higher gun elevation in order to be able to fire the shell over the longer ranges.

More men on board

The artillery gun is likely to fire for longer than a tank, expending much more ammunition. Only a limited number of rounds can actually be carried on the gun itself, and so the balance is in a separate vehicle. To maintain the rate of fire the gun needs a crew of 5 or 6, including the commander, the driver, the gun layer, the loader and the ammunition handlers.

The shells

The most common type of ammunition used by the artillery gun is the High Explosive round, which is ideal for destroying trench systems or infantry on their feet in the open. The fuze on it can be set for the round to burst in the air or on impact with the ground. Smoke rounds are also used frequently to conceal the movement of friendly armor and infantry, and by night the battlefield can be lit up with illuminating rounds. The gun will have a few anti-tank rounds, but will only fire these as a last resort in the event of a sudden enemy breakthrough.

Keeping up with the battle

The key to the effectiveness of artillery on the battlefield is quick response – the ability to bring down accurate fire, on request by armor and infantry, at a moment's notice. To do this it is organized into batteries of 6-8 guns, and while one battery moves position – to prevent the enemy locating the guns and bringing down fire on

Left The French AMX-13 light tank with its oscillating turret equipped with an autoloader. This turret is used on many other hulls.

Below The Italian OF-40, which is in service with the United Arab Emirates, firing its 105mm gun.

Bottom The French Panhard ERC90 Sagaie on parade with the Mexican Army, who call it Lynx.

them – another is static and ready to fire. Self-propelled artillery can be brought into action more quickly than towed guns, to keep up with the fast pace of mobile warfare.

A vital service

Artillery is vitally important, but Precision Guided Munitions will make it even more so, conferring upon it an altogether new role – that of an anti-armor weapon. Another revolutionary new role will be to lay minefields, by firing shells containing anti-tank mine submunitions. The complaint is often heard today that there is never enough artillery available on the battlefield. It is a cry which is likely to become louder in the future.

Specialized Armor

To defend against an attack from the air, most armored vehicles have a machine gun mounted on top, but its range is very limited and it is no match for a fast-flying jet. To provide additional cover, there is now an increasing range of specialist air defense armored vehicles. Many of these mount quick-firing cannon, and incorporate radar, which can locate targets out to ten miles. These are then tracked and the guns will automatically lock on to the aircraft, engaging it when it closes to about two miles. Some surface-to-air missile systems are also mounted on armor chassis.

Engineers

The role of engineers in war is to impede the enemy's mobility, while enhancing that of their own side. The best way to achieve the former is through minefields, and a number of basic types of armored vehicle have been adapted as minefield layers. Usually these are Armored Personnel Carriers, which have plenty of room inside to carry mines. There are also plows which can be fitted to tanks for clearing minefields. Tank chassis are also used as bridge-layers, to enable armor to cross streams and anti-tank ditches. Finally, there are a number of vehicles fitted with dozer blades and winches, built specially for engineer reconnaissance tasks.

Upper Left A Scorpion changing position. Many crewmen wear 'bone domes' to protect them when going at speed over rough terrain.

Lower Left The 90mm gunned Brazilian EE-9 Cascavel. The splashboard in the front prevents water entering the driver's compartment when swimming.

Center M3 Bradley fires a TOW missile.

Upper Right This British Scorpion crew are manning an observation post.

The commander in the field

Also important are Armored Command Vehicles. These are basically Armored Personnel Carriers fitted with mapboards and additional radios which give commanders and their staffs protection against enemy artillery fire. Also, having an armored vehicle means that if they are located by the enemy, they can pack up and move off quickly.

Rescuing the casualties

Many logistics vehicles are also armored. Ambulances, again usually based on Armored Personnel Carriers, need to go right forward to rescue the wounded. Repair and recovery vehicles also have to go up to the front line, to attend to vehicle casualties. Many of these are based on a tank chassis, which has the power to tow disabled tanks. Some artillery ammunition carriers are also armored.

The amphibians

Most light armored vehicles are able to 'swim', often with little preparation, propelled by their wheels or tracks through the water. Main battle tanks are too heavy to do this, although Soviet tanks have snorkeling equipment so that they can traverse river bottoms. This is, however, risky and many things can go wrong. A number of armored vehicles in use with marine forces are specifically designed for amphibious landings. These have a much better performance in the water than those whose primary function is on dry land.

Armor in its many forms

Many specialist vehicles are based on existing tanks, reconnaissance and infantry armored vehicles. This is a much cheaper way of producing special-to-task vehicles than designing them from scratch, and makes maintenance and the supply of spare parts very much easier. What is striking, though, is the huge range of uses to which armored vehicles are put. In spite of the ever increasing threats to armor today more, rather than less, of these essential vehicles are likely to be seen on the battlefield of tomorrow.

Above The French AML90, with 90mm gun. Several different turrets with varying armament can be mounted on this hull.

Center A French Army Panhard ERC90 Sagaie crew prepare to leave barracks.

Bottom Another French armored car is the AMX-10RC, which has a 105mm gun and is in French and Moroccan Army service.

Far Right Top A British Fox, with 30mm Rarden gun, watches for the enemy.

Far Right Bottom A wheeled APC is the French Panhard VCR, which in its basic version shown here mounts a 20mm cannon.

Right The French Creusot-Loire/
Saviem VAB wheeled APC
carries ten infantrymen and is
used by a number of African and
Middle Eastern countries.

Above The Brazilian EE-11 Urutu requires little preparation for swimming, and uses its tracks and hydrojets to give it a top speed of 6 knots in water.

Right No less than fifty countries use the US M113 APC, which has a crew of two and can carry 11 infantrymen.

Left The West German Marder Mechanized Infantry Combat Vehicle, which has a 20mm cannon. It has a crew of four and carries six infantrymen.

Left The British Ranger antipersonnel mine delivery system mounted on the FV432.

Below British Army Scorpions on an operational patrol in Belize.

Right The British Army's MCV-80 with 30mm Rarden gun will shortly enter service as an infantry combat vehicle.

Far Right An M2 Bradley being put through its paces. Very similar to the M3, it carries a total of ten men and has firing ports in the hull sides and rear.

Right The AT105 Saxon has just entered British Army service. Wheeled AFVs are often used for internal security.

Far Right Many Third World countries prefer wheeled AFVs because they are cheaper and easier to maintain. These Swiss Mowag Rolands are in Sierra Leonean service.

Above The British Army's FV432 APC has been in service for over 20 years. Some will be replaced by MCV-80, but others are likely to run on for some time to come.

Right APCs often carry infantry heavy weapons. Here a Dutch crew set up their 120mm mortar, having dismounted from their DAF YP408 wheeled APC.

Below The US FMC MICV was not taken up by the US Army but is used by the Dutch, Belgian and Philippine Armies.

Left The US M109 SP gun is used by many NATO armies.

Left The Japanese Type 74 105mm SP howitzer. The Japanese also have the more powerful Type 75 155mm.

105HSP-2

Left Artillery ammunition is heavy. This US M109 155mm round weighs over 90lbs and mechanical assistance is needed to load it into the breech.

Above Ammunition resupply is a major problem for artillery, especially when under fire. The US Field Artillery Ammunition Supply Vehicle, here replenishing an M110 8in howitzer, is one answer.

Left A 155mm self-propelled howitzer turret mounted on a Vickers Mk 3 tank chassis. This is a good way of getting further use out of obsolete tanks.

Far Left The French AMX 155mm GCT SP gun, which is in service with France, Iraq and Saudi Arabia.

149

Right SP guns do not have to have a turret as these French 155mm Mk F3 howitzers show.

Far Right The British Abbot firing on the range. It uses the FV432 APC chassis and a 105mm gun.

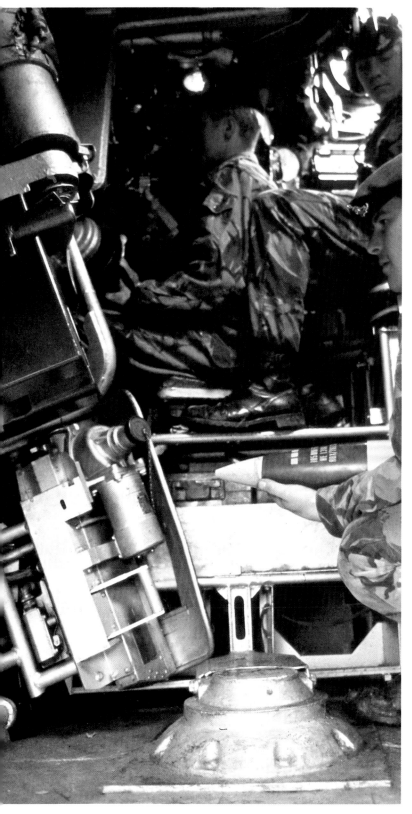

Left The interior of the British 105mm Abbot SP gun. At the top is the gun commander, to his right the gun layer, and below the loader.

Below Carrying out nuclear/chemical decontamination of an 8 inch M110 SP gun. This fires both nuclear and conventional rounds.

Left The German JPz Kanone, here in Belgian service, is not an SP artillery gun but a tank destroyer.

Below Here is the Soviet M1974 122mm SP howitzer.

Right Another of the Swiss Mowag family, the 6 x 6 Piranha, here equipped with a ground surveillance radar.

Below The British FV180 Combat Engineer Tractor. It is towing the Giant Viper mine clearance system which is based on an explosive hose.

Above Soviet ZSU-23-4 air defense vehicle, which has gained a high reputation for its effectiveness.

Top Center The Dutch version of the German Gepard, recognizable by the different radar dish shape. It is called Cheetah.

Left The West German Gepard low level air defense vehicle in action. Its radar can acquire aircraft up to five miles range and the twin 35mm cannon have an effective range of some two miles.

Left Chieftain Armored Recovery Vehicle.

Left The fully amphibious LVTP7 used by the US Marine Corps and by the Argentinians in their invasion of the Falkland Islands in 1982.

Below Left Some of the Combat Vehicle Reconnaissance (Tracked) family in British Army service – (left to right) Sultan (command), Spartan.

Above The Franco-German Roland surface-to-air missile system in action.

Left The French Thomson-CSF Sabre air defense turret mounted on a British Chieftain hull.

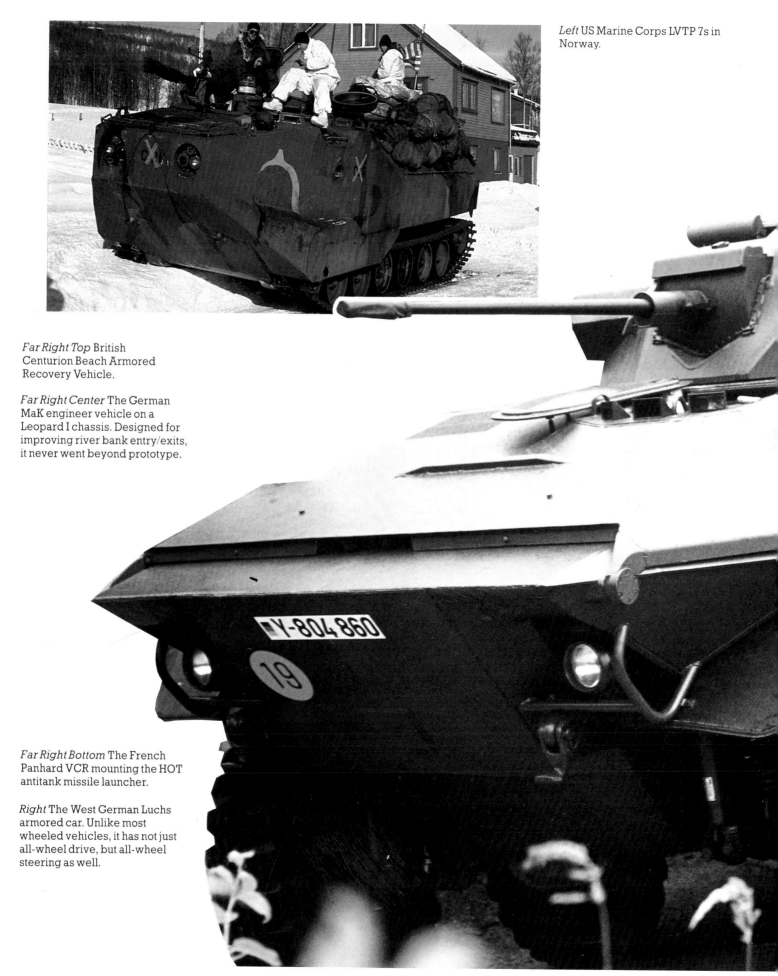

Left US Marine Corps LVTP 7s in Norway.

Far Right Top British Centurion Beach Armored Recovery Vehicle.

Far Right Center The German MaK engineer vehicle on a Leopard I chassis. Designed for improving river bank entry/exits, it never went beyond prototype.

Far Right Bottom The French Panhard VCR mounting the HOT antitank missile launcher.

Right The West German Luchs armored car. Unlike most wheeled vehicles, it has not just all-wheel drive, but all-wheel steering as well.

GUNS

A ·50 caliber machine gun atop a M1 Abrams tank. US Army, West Germany 1984.

Introduction

There is an amazing variety of guns, ranging from the hand-held small arms which are the weapons of the infantry, to the monstrous artillery weapons that require many men and considerable logistical organization for them to play a decisive part on the battlefield.

Small arms are personal weapons designed to aid the user in the offensive and defensive operations, but the category also includes the machine-gun, which comes in different calibers and weights to suit the needs of small bodies of infantrymen. Artillery comprises those heavier weapons that fire shells rather than shot and need a crew to serve them.

The two types of gun are similar in their method of operation. They are both essentially breech-loaded rifled tubes designed to eject a projectile under the pressure of rapidly-burning propellant, that generates a large volume of gas between the projectile and the breech. This basic design configuration was fixed in the last quarter of the nineteenth century, and though modern weapons in both categories may not resemble their ancestors of a hundred years ago the operating principles and layout remain in essence unaltered

Personal weapons: rifles and pistols

The smallest and probably least useful of small arms is the pistol. This is now reserved for officers and non-commissioned officers on the battlefield, but is more generally carried by rear-echelon troops and specialists such as aircrew, engineers and military police.

The revolver was much favored in the opening decades of this century. Its rotating magazine (generally holding six rounds) provided a useful multi-shot capability for close-quarter fighting, and its mechanical simplicity made it reliable on the varied terrains over which most armies had to fight. During and after World War II, the revolver's popularity was overtaken by that of the automatic pistol, a more compact weapon holding more rounds, whose self-reloading capability offered useful combat advantages over the revolver.

Pistols such as the FN-Browning, Beretta, Tokarev and Walther have now joined older types such as the Colt, Luger and Mauser as favorite weapons. It can rightly be argued that the pistol is an inefficient weapon even at close quarters, but it is also a potent morale-booster and will probably remain in service for some decades to come.

The long rifle

Far more effective than the pistol as a personal weapon is the rifle, the standard weapon of the infantryman. By the middle of last century, rifled weapons had been produced that were capable of firing accurately over ranges of 500 yards or more. These rifles however were limited by the fact that they were single-shot weapons.

This made reloading comparatively slow. It also meant that the rifle had to be taken away from the firer's shoulder, reloaded and then aimed again.

By the end of the century these problems had been overcome. The sliding-bolt action did away with the need to remove the rifle from the shoulder and the adoption of a magazine under the bolt action meant that rapid fire could be maintained for several rounds (up to 10 in some British weapons). Moreover, the evolution of nitrocellulose propellants produced higher velocities (and hence flatter and more accurate firing trajectories) without the cloud of black smoke associated with gunpowder weapons; and the development of modern machining processes and sights combined to make possible accurate fire at ranges of some 1,000 yards when the weapon was handled by a marksman.

The rifles that resulted from these developments were some of the classics of the military gunsmith's art: the M1903 Springfield in the US, the Short Magazine, Lee-Enfield in Britain and the Mauser Gewehr 98 in Germany. With these weapons, trained infantry could fire perhaps 15 to 20 aimed rounds per minute, picking off an advancing enemy at long range. At close range, in either offense or defense, the long rifles could be fitted with fearsome sword bayonets, turning them into extemporized pikes with a reach of some 6 ft.

The changing character of war

But no sooner had these weapons been developed and blooded in a variety of colonial wars than World War I began and made them obsolete. The ghastly trench warfare that characterized this conflict showed that the full-length military rifle was of only limited use. With exceptions such as the Battle of Mons and desert warfare in Mesopotamia, long-range accurate fire was neither possible nor useful, and the longer rifles were a decided disadvantage in the trenches of the Western Front because of their unwieldiness. What was needed were shorter weapons designed to fire accurately over ranges of only some 250 yards but with a far higher rate of fire and the reliability to operate with minimum maintenance under the most difficult conditions of mud, dust, sand and snow.

It took a long time for these weapons to evolve, however, largely because of the entrenched position of authorities who favored the accurate rifle firing a powerful round. They claimed — quite rightly — that shorter weapons, such as the carbine, were difficult to handle because of their savage recoil, but refused to consider the adoption of a less powerful round on the grounds that it would not be a 'man-stopper'. With the notable exception of the British, who had found a nice balance with the SMLE, the world thus moved toward medium-length rifles with self-reloading capability. A classic example was the M1 Garand, used by the US Army during World War II, which retained the standard US rifle caliber of 0.3 inches.

Above Right The classic German infantry rifle of World War II was the 7.92-mm Gewehr 98k, adopted in 1935 as a shorter-length version of the overlong Gewehr 98 pattern rifle.

Right Substantially unchanged from the time of its service debut in 1941, the British Rifle No. 4 was a 0.303-in weapon, and is here seen with a spike bayonet.

Below Left Of full-powered military rifles in current service, one of the most popular and effective is the 7.62-mm FN FAL, designed in Belgium but used in very substantial numbers in a variety of forms all over the world.

Bottom Left The British version of the FAL is the L1A1 made by the Royal Small Arms Factory at Enfield and by the Royal Ordnance Factory at Fazackerley. The L1A1 is no longer in production and is about to be replaced by the 4.85-mm Individual Weapon.

Above One of the oddities of US weapon procurement in World War II was the Carbine M1, seen here being carried by the point man of this patrol. Though chambered in the standard 0.3in, this weapon fired a low-powered round of limited range.

Below Undoubtedly the most widely used military weapon in the world is the Soviet-designed AK-47 assault rifle, which is chambered for an intermediate-power 7.62-mm round and is notable for its high rate of fire and extreme sturdiness. The taped-together magazines allow end-for-end magazine changes with minimum delay on the battlefield.

The assault rifle

World War II reinforced the lessons of World War I, and in its closing stages there at last began to appear what are now called assault rifles, designed specifically for the modern battlefield's short-range and high-volume fire requirements. The distinctive features of these new weapons, epitomized by the German Sturmgewehr 44, were simplicity of design and manufacture, with emphasis on low-cost stampings and pressings rather than costly and time-consumptive machined parts; semi-automatic and automatic fire capabilities; intermediate-power ammunition comprising a rifle-caliber projectile with a reduced propellant load, contained in a large and easily-changed magazine (20 or more rounds); and general optimization for rapid fire at close range.

Operational analysis showed that the average infantryman of World War II only very rarely used the aimed-fire capabilities of his rifle, and so the assault rifle, able to produce large volumes of poorly-aimed fire was soon deemed to offer greater battlefield capability than the rifle. The assault rifle came into its own with weapons such as the Soviet AK-47, its successor the AKM, and the Israeli Galil. The Western world was slightly slower on the uptake. They first adopted semi-automatic weapons with a full-power round, but of compact and relatively lightweight design, a large magazine and short-range sights, such as the American M14, Belgian FN FAL and German Heckler and Koch G-3, before moving to weapons like the American M16. This has 5.56 in. caliber, and full automatic capability in a design using composite structure and a large magazine.

'Straight through' weapons

Currently, there is a move towards an even lighter weapon, but one still designed to produce masses of fire over short ranges. These are the so-called 'straight-through' weapons, built to a concept that takes the weapon in a straight line from the buttplate to the muzzle for ease of sighting and handling. Composite materials are commonly used in these new weapons, which also feature small-caliber lightweight ammunition so that the infantryman can carry many more rounds. Other possible advances, are caseless rounds, whose solid propellant will do away with the comparatively heavy brass case of standard rounds and the need to extract the spent case before a fresh round is chambered; and projectiles with better ballistic qualities. Allied to these improvements are better sights of the image-intensifying type, making it possible for the infantryman to operate effectively in mist and at night.

Above Far Left No matter how well designed it is, any military weapon relies for battlefield reliability on simple maintenance and the cleanliness and free movement of its working parts.

Above Left The use of small-caliber ammunition and composite materials has done much to reduce the size and weight of service weapons, making it possible even for children to use rifles such as the US 5.56-mm M16A1, a practice common in regions where irregular warfare is endemic.

Left West Germany's equivalent of the FAL is the 7.62-mm G3.

Above Top, Right The USA's standard service rifle is the lightweight M16A1, evolved after nearly disastrous teething problems with the M16.

Above Right, Center The relatively light and compact M16A1 is ideally suited to the need of the USA's slightly-built allies in Asia, and is also admirably sized for jungle operations.

Right The Israeli Galil 5.56-mm assault rifle is an extremely versatile weapon, and can be fitted with a folding stock and a bipod that doubles as a wire-cutter.

Above Set to become one of the most important handguns in the world is the Beretta Model 92F, developed in Italy and adopted early in 1985 as the US forces' standard automatic pistol as a replacement for the venerable Colt M1911A1. The Model 92F fires a standard 9-mm Parabellum round, and the magazine holds 15 rounds.

Left Primary requirements for any modern military weapon are extremely robust construction, small overall size, light weight, and a careful combination of ammunition and sights for maximum battlefield ranges in the order of some 400 m.

Below A useful combination weapon (front foreground) is the 5.56-mm M16A1 rifle fitted under the forebody with an M203 grenade launcher designed to fire the extensive range of 40-mm combat grenades.

Above Left Widely used in its AK-47 and AKM forms, the Soviet Kalashnikov assault rifle is used by all armies and paramilitary forces supplied by the USSR. This Arab guerrilla has a weapon modified to launch rifle grenades, while the man in the background has an RPG-7 anti-tank launcher.

Left The Galil is an extraordinarily versatile weapon, and though used mainly as an assault rifle it can also be deployed as a sub-machine gun, a light machine-gun, and a grenade launcher for anti-tank and anti-personnel weapons.

Far Left Seen with bipod legs folded forward under the barrel, the FR-F1 is the standard French sniper rifle, and is typical of current bolt-action sniping rifles. The weapon is chambered for the full-power 7.5-mm rifle round, and comes with a modèle 53 bis telescopic sight, long barrel and cheek piece. The magazine holds 10 rounds.

Above Combat troops are as much in favour of camouflaging their weapons (M16A1 rifles) as themselves.

Left Typical of the new generation of small-caliber straight-through weapon designs is the French FA MAS personal weapon. Chambered for the 5.56-mm round, this lightweight weapon can produce semi-automatic, automatic and burst fire, and it carries 25 rounds in the magazine. A grenade launcher can also be fitted.

Sub-machine guns and machine guns

At first called a machine-pistol, the sub-machine gun resulted directly from the trench warfare of World War I. Early weapons such as the German Bergmann and Italian Revelli were all attempts to provide trench-bound infantry with a handy gun able to produce large volumes of fire for close-range engagements. The result was a light and comparatively short weapon design for fully-automatic fire, with pistol ammunition accommodated in a large magazine.

Development continued with nicely engineered weapons such as the American Thompson, in the period between the World Wars, but the type came of age in World War II, with much cheaper weapons produced from stampings and pressings. Typical of these were the British Sten, the American M3, the German MP38 and MP40 and the Soviet PPSh and PPS. They were later succeeded by the still-current British Sterling, French MAT 49 and Israeli Uzi weapon. As a type, however, the sub-machine gun has been largely supplanted by the assault rifle, which combines the best attributes of rifle and sub-machine gun in a single design, with obvious advantages in training, procurement and ammunition supply.

Early machine guns

The machine-gun is the natural partner to the rifle. In defense its fully-automatic fire can rain down on attackers from a distance, while in offense it can keep the enemy occupied as the infantry advances. Military commanders had desired such a weapon long before the Gatling gun first made its appearance in the 1860s. But the Gatling was a cumbersome device that needed an external power source — hand cranking — to operate it, and so was very limited in its tactical applications.

The first truly practical machine-gun was demonstrated some 20 years later. This was the Maxim, which used the recoil force of one round to unlock the gun's breech, extract the spent round, cock the mechanism and chamber the next round; making possible a high cyclic rate of fire so long as the weapon could be cooled and fed with ammunition. Water- and air-cooled versions of the Maxim were very quickly adopted by all the modern armies of the day, and the gun was used to great effect during the Russo-Japanese War of 1904-5.

Above Right The MP40 was a classic World War II sub-machine gun, and made use of stamped instead of machined parts, for ease of production, wherever possible. Caliber was 9-mm, and the magazine held 32 rounds. The MP40 can be truly regarded as the first 'modern' sub-machine gun.

Right Typical of current sub-machine guns is the Swedish 9-mm Model 45, physically reminiscent of the British Sten but with an angular folding stock and a 36-round two-column box magazine.

Above Left Perhaps the best-known modern sub-machine gun is the Israeli Uzi. Fitted with a retractable stock, this is an exceptionally compact weapon, and among its many virtues is the capability to take box magazines holding 25, 32 or 64 rounds of 9-mm Parabellum ammunition. The weapon's small size and low weight have made it popular with special forces, paramilitary units and police forces, and the type has been widely exported as well as being made under license.

Left Though the sub-machine gun has lost ground as a 'conventional' military weapon, it still has a role to play in modern military operations, especially in the context of urban combat, as exemplified by this 9-mm Sterling L2A3 in the hands of this British soldier.

Opposite Page, Top Left The sub-machine gun (here a Sterling L2A3) is still popular with élite forces such as the British Parachute Regiment.

Opposite Page, Top Right A machine-gun that can truly claim to have made history is the German 7.92-mm MG34, seen here in the context of the Mediterranean theater in World War II. Extremely reliable and comparatively light as it was an air-cooled weapon, the MG34 was accurate and possessed an extremely high rate of fire, and could be used as a medium or light machine-gun with a tripod or bipod mounting respectively.

Opposite Page, Bottom Perhaps the best British machine-gun of World War II, the 0.303-in Bren Gun was a light machine-gun evolved at Enfield from the Czech Brno-designed ZGB. The Bren was light, accurate and fired from a 30-round curved box magazine above the receiver.

Above Left An MG34 is seen in the sustained-fire role on a tripod mounting. The weapon could remain in action virtually as long as ammunition could be supplied.

Left The classic machine-gun of World War II was the MG42, based mechanically on the MG34 but simplified in construction to make greater use of pressings and stamped parts in place of machined units. From the MG42 can be traced the development of many modern air-cooled machine-guns.

Top The Belgian-designed FN MAG may be considered the automatic counterpart of the FAL rifle, and has been widely exported as a medium and heavy machine-gun in 7.62-mm caliber.

Above Introduced in 1933 and still the doyen of heavy machine-guns, the Browning M2 0.5-in weapon is extremely effective against surface and low-flying aerial targets, and can fire a variety of ammunition types at a cyclic rate of some 550 rounds per minute.

Right One of the great virtues of the general-purpose machine-gun is its combination of portability and high rate of fire when used with belt-fed ammunition. These features make such guns a favorite with irregular forces.

Above The version of the MAG used by the British forces is the L7A2, seen here in the light machine-gun role on a bipod mount. Belt-fed, the weapon has a normal operational rate of fire of 25 rounds per minute, rising to 100 rounds per minute in the rapid-fire regime, compared with 100 and 200 rounds per minute respectively in the sustained-fire role. The cyclic rate of the weapon is between 750 and 1,000 rounds per minute.

Left The sustained-fire role of the L7A2 is made more effective by the use of the Tripod Mounting, 7.62-mm MG, L4A1. This allows all-round traverse and elevation between −11° and +22°. The use of a sight identical with that fitted to the 81-mm mortar allows the weapon to be used for accurately-laid indirect fire.

Right Just as the MAG is the machine-gun equivalent to the FAL rifle, the Soviet 7.62-mm PK series is the machine-gun counterpart to the AK series assault rifle, and has been extensively supplied to Soviet allies and clients in all parts of the world. The basic PK and tripod-mounted PKS have fluted barrels, while the later PKM and tripod-mounted PKMS have plain barrels, and the PKB (or PKMB) has spade grips in the manner of many sustained-fire weapons.

Below Now entering widespread production, the FN Minimi, epitomises the new generation of 5.56-mm light machine-guns, with multiple feed options and great battlefield portability.

Center Left In the sustained-fire role and mounted on its tripod mounting, the L7A2 is often used without its butt, the gunner using the pistol grip, by the trigger assembly, for the effective control of his weapon.

Right and Below Of much the same design vintage as the Browning M2, the Soviet 12.7-mm Degtyarev heavy machine-gun series (whose best-known members are the Models 1938 and Model 38/46) lacks the flair and versatility of the American weapon, but continues in service with many armies and irregular forces a light anti-armor and anti-tank weapon, in the former role using the Model 1943 AA sight shown (right).

The battlefields of Europe

By 1914 there were two basic types of machine-gun in use: the air-cooled light machine-gun with drum magazine for mobile use, on a bipod mounting, and the water-cooled heavy machine-gun with belt magazine for the sustained-fire role, on a tripod mounting. Both types were generally found in the same calibers as standard service rifles. Quite soon, however, it became clear that the sheer weight of water-cooled weapons was a great tactical disadvantage, and so air-cooled medium machine-guns were developed. All three types were extensively used in World War I and, together with barbed wire, became the decisive weapons of the battlefields on the Western and other fronts. Typical of the light machine-guns were the Lewis gun and German MG08/15, of the medium machine-guns the American Browning M1919 and French Hotchkiss, and of the heavy machine-guns the British Vickers and the German MG08. Development along these lines continued in the period between the World Wars with such classics as the American M2 heavy machine-gun and the Czech Brno ZB26, developed by the British into the Bren light machine-gun.

The world's first effective general-purpose machine-gun was the German MG34. This was a belt- or magazine-fed air-cooled weapon with a prodigiously high rate of fire, and capable of operation on a bipod for tactical deployment, or on a tripod for sustained fire. Still more advanced was the MG42, which retained all the advantages of the earlier MG34 but was easier and less costly to produce.

Modern developments

The MG42, which is still in service today in a number of guises, spurred a period of rapid evolution in machine-gun design, leading in the 1950s to the adoption almost worldwide of the general-purpose machine-gun as a belt-fed tactical weapon. Typical of these are the British L7, the American M60 and the Soviet PK.

Experience has shown that for all its logistic advantages, the use of only a general-purpose machine-gun has tactical drawbacks, not least the weight of the weapon on a mobile battlefield, but also the difficulty of supplying belted ammunition in adequate quantities. Of late, therefore, the light machine-gun has reappeared, usually a derivative of the standard assault rifle with a heavier barrel, but retaining a magazine. One example of this type is the Ultimax 100 from Singapore, generally claimed as the world's lightest machine-gun, and designed like others of this class for the squad automatic weapon role. Such weapons are now beginning to enter widespread service. Perhaps the most important of them is the Belgian FN Minimi, which uses standard 5.56mm ammunition like the Ultimax, and has been adopted by the US Army.

Cannon and Mortar

The cannon is distinguished from the machine-gun by the fact that its ammunition carries an explosive payload, of which the smallest caliber that is practical is 20mm. The need for such weapons was first experienced during World War I, as a defense against low-flying aircraft. During the inter-war period the most important cannon types developed were the 20mm Oerlikon from Switzerland and the 40mm Bofors from Sweden. Both were very widely used in World War II by both sides, the Bofors being developed with proximity-fused shells and radar-directed power mountings. Since then, the cannon has continued to develop as a low-level AA defense weapon, with both Bofors and Oerlikon, as well as Rheinmetall of West Germany, in the forefront. Calibers from 20 to 40mm are now in widespread service in a variety of computerized and optical mountings, all powered for rapid traverse and elevation. These have proved devastating in Vietnam and the Middle East, especially cannon in multiple mountings such as the Soviet 23mm ZU-23.

Far Left The problem of countering sea-skimming anti-ship missiles has led to the development of specialized close-in weapon systems: these combine a Gatling-type heavy cannon, radars and a computer fire-control system for a high hit probability in minimum time. Seen here is the Dutch Goalkeeper system with a General Electric cannon and Hollandse Signaalapparaten radars.

Opposite Page, Bottom The American counterpart of the Goalkeeper system is the Phalanx system using a 20-mm M61 Vulcan cannon rather than the Goalkeeper's 30-mm GAU-8/A weapon.

Left Essentially an interim weapon, the US M163 land-mobile AA system combines a Vulcan cannon, its feed system, a fire-control system and a range-only radar on an M113 armored personnel carrier hull. However, the weapon lacks the traverse and elevation rates to deal with low-level targets moving at high speeds, and the armament system lacks protection.

Center Left A potent towed AA system is the Greek Artemis, which combines two 30-mm Mauser Model F cannon with the options of remote radar control, or powered operation by a centrally-seated gunner, or emergency manual operation by the gunner.

Left The ZU-23 was designed and produced in the USSR, and has been widely exported. The two 23-mm cannon are powerful AA weapons.

Above Though obsolete, the ZPU-4 mounting with a quartet of 14.5-mm machine-guns is still encountered in Africa, Asia and the Middle East.

179

Mortars

Technically, mortars are not guns, since they are muzzle-loaded rather than breech-loaded weapons. They are however, included here for the sake of completeness. Like many modern weapons, the mortar has its origins in World War I, but was first developed as a useful tactical weapon in the inter-war period. It consisted of a tube, moveable in elevation and azimuth, above a substantial baseplate which fired finned bombs for plunging fire onto an enemy at a range of between a few hundred to a few thousand yards.

The mortar breaks down into components for easy transport by infantry, and is designed for infantry support. Calibers range from 51 to 81mm in this basic support role, in which smoke, illuminating flares and other rounds can be fired as well as HE (high explosive). For specialist roles, heavier models are used, including the American 4.2in., the French 120mm and Soviet 240mm weapons. The last named is apparently capable of firing a low-yield nuclear weapon. The primary functional characteristic of mortars is their very steep trajectory, making them highly effective against entrenched positions. Current research is centered on the development of 'smart' munitions with infra-red or radar seekers to permit mortars to engage tanks from vertically above, the tank's weakest quadrant.

Above Right Manually operated, and thus comparatively slow in elevation and traverse, the Soviet ZPU-4 mounting has a four-barrel cyclic rate of 2,400 rounds per minute, though a more practical rate is 600 rounds per minute. Some 4,800 rounds are carried.

Right Though obsolete by the latest criteria, the twin-barrel ZPU-2 14.5-mm AA mounting can still find effective use in areas such as Afghanistan.

Below Right The M163 tracked Vulcan system can traverse and elevate at 60° and 45° per second respectively, and the cannon has two fire rates: 1,000 rounds per minute against ground targets and 3,000 rounds per minute against air targets. Bursts of 10, 30, 60 or 100 rounds can be selected.

Opposite Page, Top Typical of modern anti-tank recoilless rifles is the 84-mm Carl Gustav designed in Sweden. This can achieve some six shots per minute, and the FFV 551 round can penetrate 400 mm of armor at ranges up to 500 m.

Opposite Page, Bottom Mounted in converted armored personnel carriers, mortars are ideal weapons for the modern mobile battlefield.

Right Apart from its high-angle fire and pinpoint accuracy, the British 81-mm and other mortars have the added advantage of great tactical versatility through being able to fire rounds such as HE, smoke, incendiary, illuminating and the like. There is now the possibility of 'smart' munitions able to home onto targets pinpointed in flight.

Below British paratroops with an 81-mm L16 mortar. Like comparable weapons, the L16 breaks down into three loads (barrel, baseplate and tripod) for manpacking.

Above One of the smallest mortars in current service is the Spanish Commando Model C, a 60-mm weapon carried and used by one man, whereas most 81-mm weapons are operated by three men.

Left The type of artillery that has now completely disappeared from the scene is epitomized by the Germans' World War II 21-cm Kanone 12 (Eisenbahn), an 8.3-in railway gun able to lob a 237-lb shell over a range of 71.5 miles. Extraordinarily expensive in production and operation, such guns were wholly cost-*in*effective.

Artillery in the field

Crew-served artillery is divided into two basic categories: the gun and the howitzer. The gun is designed to engage the target with direct fire, and thus does not elevate to more than +45°, whereas the howitzer, which is designed for indirect-fire engagements, fires its projectile at an elevation of more than +45° to produce plunging fire. Much of the efficiency of the gun's projectile is derived from its kinetic effect (momentum), so the shells fired by guns tend to contain more metal and less explosive than the shell fired from a howitzer of the same caliber, whose projectile has a lower terminal velocity and thus works better with an HE rather than kinetic effect.

The beginnings

Modern artillery may be said to have begun with the great French '75', the 75mm field gun introduced in 1897. Until then, artillery pieces had possessed only the crudest buffer system between the ordnance (gun) and its carriage, so that after every discharge the gun had to be relaid in azimuth and elevation because the whole carriage recoiled with the gun when it was fired. The '75' displayed an effective system of buffers and recuperators, to control the recoil of the ordnance on the carriage and to bring the ordnance back to its original position without the carriage being disturbed, ready for reloading. Because of this, the '75' achieved unprecedented rates of fire, and the buffer/recuperator system was soon adopted worldwide. Even today, technical improvements have not altered the basic concept.

Hybrid artillery

Guns and howitzers were very widely used in both World Wars: guns, normally for the engagement of targets such as tanks and pillboxes, and howitzers for targets buried under earth or concrete or hidden from direct engagement behind a hill. World War I artillery ranged in caliber from some 75 to 150mm for the medium pieces, while the artillery used in World War II was of slightly larger caliber, from 85 to 155mm.

World War II also saw the emergence of a hybrid artillery type, the gun/howitzer, which had a barrel length of somewhere between the short barrel of the howitzer and the long barrel of the gun, and was capable of elevation from −5° to +45°. Like other artillery pieces of the period, the gun/howitzer often had a turntable for rapid 360° traverse, and could fire ammunition varying from solid armor-piercing shot to HE. A variety of other artillery types also emerged in World War II. These included specialized anti-tank guns of low silhouette and very high muzzle velocity; rapid-firing anti-aircraft guns such as the magnificent German 88mm series, which also proved potent in an anti-tank role.

Left Infantry defence against armored vehicles is now the responsibility mainly of guided missiles. Though these are potent weapons, their primary failings are slow speed and the backblast on firing, which make missile and launch-team detection comparatively simple, with unfortunate consequences.

Left Produced jointly by Italy, the UK and West Germany, the FH-70 155-mm howitzer is typical of modern towed field artillery. It is fitted with an auxiliary power unit for local movement, and can fire a 43.5-kg projectile to a range of 24,000 m, increasing to 30,000 m when a rocket-assisted projectile is used.

Below Left The British 5.5-in gun-howitzer was a good weapon of its type in World War II, being a versatile weapon with adequate cross-country towing performance. Against it, however, were its non-standard calibre and very considerable weight.

Right, Above The British 105-mm Light Gun is a good example of modern towed ordnance. It can be used for direct and indirect fire, and is light enough for simple air transport with additional battlefield mobility provided by helicopter lift. A 35.5-lb projectile can be fired to 17,200 m.

Right, Below Though fitted with an auxiliary power unit for independent local movement, the 155-mm FH-77A Swedish howitzer is normally towed by a truck. Note the ammunition crane for a more rapid rate of fire.

Far Left Modern artillery is characterized by a wide diversity of projectile types, including terminally-guided and submunition-carrying types, produced to very high standards of uniformity for consistent performances.

Left The Bofors FH-77A 155-mm howitzer in action during a Swedish exercise. The loading arrangements of this massive weapon make possible bursts of three shells in six to eight seconds.

Below, Far Left The largest piece of towed artillery in service, the US 8-in M115 howitzer was introduced in 1940, and is a massive weapon weighing in at 32,000 lb. Maximum range is only 18,400 yards because of the short barrel, and among the projectile inventory are HE, chemical and nuclear rounds.

Below Left For stability reasons on its light carriage, the 105-mm Light Gun is restricted in traverse to 5.5° left and right, though the use of a turntable means that the whole equipment can easily be slewed by manpower onto the right bearing when target has to be shifted.

Bottom The curved trails and turntable of the 105-mm Light Gun are evident in this rear view of the excellent weapon.

Right Well able to deliver several projectile types over long ranges, the FH-70 howitzer has a crew of eight, and has on-carriage traverse and elevation of 56° and −5°/+70° respectively. Though bursts of three rounds in 13 seconds are possible, the more normal rate is six rounds per minute.

Below When obsolete by the standards of the leading powers, older artillery weapons often remain in service in the remoter parts of the world.

Bottom Tube-launched 'smart' projectiles are the up-and-coming thing in artillery circles, this being the American Copperhead anti-tank round with laser homing.

Left Last-ditch anti-tank defense of infantry positions is undertaken by one-shot disposable rocket-launchers, such as the West German Armbrust. This can deliver a HEAT warhead over a range of some 300 m with useful accuracy, and the warhead can penetrate some 300 mm of armor at that range.

Below Left Cheaper to build and more versatile in operation than tube artillery, the multiple rocket-launcher is coming to the fore as a saturation weapon also able to deliver mines and even guided submunitions. This is the American MLRS.

Below The moment of firing. Many modern artillery weapons have radar equipment to give an exact muzzle velocity reading for the accurate elevation of the barrel for the next round.

Right The wrong end of an American M198 155-mm howitzer. Modern technology, especially in the fields of materials and munitions, has enabled towed artillery to remain viable at a time when self-propelled weapons seemed likely to dominate.

Below and Opposite Page Developed by Vought for the US Army and in the process of large-scale procurement for this and other land forces, the MLRS was conceived as a low-cost conventional means of offsetting any enemy's massive superiority in armor strength. Typical of the offensive load carried by an MLRS rocket is the nest of 644 M77 dual-role shaped-charge blast/fragmentation bomblets designed to cover a large area with anti-tamper weapons able to penetrate 100-mm of armor.

PICTURE CREDITS